SHARKS!

Piero and Alberto Angela
Alberto Luca Recchi

SHARKS!

Predators of the Sea

COURAGE
BOOKS
AN IMPRINT OF RUNNING PRESS
PHILADELPHIA · LONDON

Page 1: A "mermaid's purse": the egg case with embryo of a swellshark.

Pages 2–3: Underwater plants, including seaweed and sea tangle (genus *Laminaria*), just beneath the surface.

Pages 4–5: Caribbean reef sharks (*Carcharhinus perezi*) have spotted a wounded tuna.

Pages 6–7: The oceanic white tip (*Carcharhinus longimanus*)—beautiful, elegant, and extremely aggressive.

Pages 8: The tiger shark (*Galeocerdo cuvier*), with a flat, broad nose and a bottomless mouth.

Right: For reasons still unknown, whale sharks (*Rhincodon typus*) like these gather off the western coasts of Australia. They are so large that planes can spot them from the air and radio their position to boats carrying tourists and scuba divers. The boats are then able to find and observe the sharks.

All of the photographs in this book, including those on the cover, by Alberto Luca Recchi

Text by Piero and Alberto Angela and Alberto Luca Recchi

Art Director: Giorgio Seppi

Design: Roberta Merlo

Editor: Adriana Savorani

Cover: Cristina Bazzoni

Published by Courage Books
Copyright © 1997 by Arnoldo Mondadori Editore, S.p.A.
English translation © 1997 by Arnoldo Mondadori Editore, S.p.A. All rights reserved.

9 8 7 6 5 4 3 2 1
Digit on the right indicates the number of this printing

Library of Congress Cataloging-in-Publication Number 97-77495

ISBN 0-7624-0354-3

Published by Courage Books, an imprint of Running Press Book Publishers
125 South Twenty-second Street
Philadelphia, Pennsylvania 19103-4399

Printed and bound in Spain by Artes Gráficas Toledo, S.A.
D.L. TO: 259-1998

Contents

13 THE PREDATORS OF THE SEA
14 The attack
22 "White death"

27 ANATOMY OF A MURDERER
28 What is a shark?
31 An oversize liver
34 Jet or pump-action?
38 Hydrodynamics
50 Turbo
54 A swimming mouth
71 From egg to umbilicus

77 THE SEVEN SENSES
78 Long-distance sensing
82 Shark eyes
87 Electric smell
90 The body tongue

95 PREY
96 Ambush on the high seas
102 A stomach of iron

111 SHARKS AND PEOPLE
112 Sharkphobia
114 Protecting people
123 A predator in danger

127 ONCE UPON A TIME
128 Distant origins
134 What remains

138 Bibliography and acknowledgments
139 The magnificent twelve
140 Index of names

The predators of the sea

B aker's Beach, San Francisco, May 7, 1959. Low on the horizon, the setting sun casts a warm glow across the waters of the Pacific Ocean. It seems like a magical moment for a swim, and Shirley O'Neil and her fiancé, Albert Kogler, decide to take a brief dip in the water just offshore. They reach a point only a few hundred feet from the beach and swim slowly along, chatting back and forth in the pink light of the sunset. Shirley is swimming a short distance ahead of Albert when suddenly she hears him scream.

She turns in time to see the shape of a giant shark slice through the water between herself and her fiancé. Albert is very much aware of his desperate situation. In an attempt to save Shirley he screams across the water to her, "It's a shark! It's a shark! Get away!"

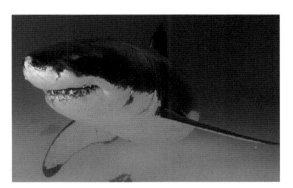

• **The attack**
• **"White death"**

The attack

The shark slams into the man like a torpedo, and the water fills with blood. But the man is still alive and screaming. Shirley hesitates a moment—she knows she is in enormous danger, but doesn't try to get away. As she explains later, "I knew I couldn't leave him. It was terrible. I could tell that the shark was biting him, and his screams were horrible. He was calling out for help." By then the water all around them is blood red, and she can no longer see the shark. With enormous courage she moves forward and tries to grab Albert's hand. One of his arms has been nearly torn from his body; Shirley grabs him from behind. As she does so she discovers the terrible, gaping wounds in his body. Shirley and Albert begin making their way back toward shore, but it is a race against time—he has already lost a great deal of blood, is growing weaker, and the shark could attack again at any moment. Shirley struggles to get him safely back to shore. By the time they finally reach the shallow water and then the beach, other people have arrived and rush to help them.

But it's too late. The loss of blood and shock prove too much, and Albert dies on the beach in the light of the last rays of the sun. Shirley, however, is unharmed. As so often happens in cases like this, the shark did not attack the rescuer, but unleashed its fury only on its victim. This was in 1959, and the shark responsible for the attack was never captured. Many suspect it must have been a great white shark (*Carcharodon carcharias*), for they often visit these waters in search of sea lions. The white shark is one of the most dangerous species, in fact the only one to which the term "man-eater" can be correctly applied.

It's a commonly accepted "fact" that any encounter with a shark will end in tragedy. The image of the shark varies little in newspapers, television, movies, and popular novels: it is always a mindless killer, ready to attack any unfortunate swimmer or diver. The story of Shirley and Albert, which appeared on the front pages of newspapers for several days, only reinforced this opinion. The reality, however, is much different. Of the more than 370 species of shark, only a very few are dangerous

Preceding pages and these pages: Examples of great white sharks (*Carcharodon carcharias*). As they age, the bodies of these sharks become increasingly covered with deep gashes and scars, a result of battles with prey and with other sharks. As signs of age, these scars can be compared to the wrinkles on human skin.

Far left: Whale shark (*Rhincodon typus*). *Left:* Stingray (*Dasyatis sp.*). *Below:* The Caribbean reef shark (*Carcharhinus perezi*). Although they must swim to breathe, sharks need not be perpetually on the move. In fact, many sharks lie motionless on the bottom or rest suspended in the water. The reef shark, in particular, can be found resting in underwater caves, apparently "asleep."

to humans. But these few "killers" have ruined the reputation of these splendid predators. Lions, tigers, and leopards are also seriously dangerous animals, but no one would think of calling a house cat a killer. In a certain sense, the same thing applies to sharks, the difference being that the "house cats" of the shark world make up fully 90 percent of the species, and the real "beasts" only the remaining 10 percent. Of course, even a relatively harmless shark like a tope or a nurse shark (a kind that scuba divers often pet) can become dangerous if provoked. Out of self-defense they might even bite, just like any other animal that feels threatened, from a turtle to a canary. The situation is much different with those species of shark that will attack a human or a boat without provocation. Species like the great white (*Carcharodon carcharias*), mako (*Isurus oxyrinchus*), tiger shark (*Galeocerdo cuvier*), bull shark (*Carcharhinus leucas*), great hammerhead (*Sphyrina mokarran*), blue shark (*Prionace glauca*), or oceanic white tip (*Carcharhinus longimanus*) are, or can quickly become, extremely dangerous. These are the sharks involved in most attacks on humans.

The world inhabited by sharks is so vast that it is difficult to imagine how it could be more varied: it ranges from the warm waters off tropical isles to the icy seas around Greenland. It also extends from waters at the surface, illuminated and warmed by the sun, down to the cold, dark depths of the abyss, and from the rolling waves of coral reefs to the motionless, muddy bottoms of sea floors. To live in such a variety of environments sharks have had to adapt in a number of ways: water temperature, degree of salinity, luminosity, and even the amount of oxygen change at the various "levels" of the ocean. Some sharks are as flat as rays. They live on ocean bottoms and eat small fish or crustaceans. Others are enormous, sometimes as long as a city bus. Fortunately, these are "gentle giants," and they eat only plankton. Other sharks are so small they can be easily held in the palm of a hand. There are sharks whose bodies seem to display obvious adaptations. For example, there are those with "wings" at the sides of the head—their eyes and nostrils are located on the tips of these "wings," perhaps to make them more effective, or perhaps to help the sharks swim. These sharks are the so-called hammerheads (*Sphyrina zygaena*), which spend most of their time near the surface. Another shark whose body seems to indicate a special adaptation is the thresher (*Alopias vulpinas*). The upper lobe of its tail is greatly elongated, nearly doubling the length of its body: it is believed that this tail is used to herd together the small fish on which the shark feeds or to slap the water to frighten the fish. Surprises in the shark world do not end there. Some sharks live in rivers, swimming hundreds of miles up their lengths. This is the case with the bull or Zambezi shark (*Carcharhinus leucas*), one of the most dangerous species. It lives primarily in the western Atlantic but can be found even in the Mississippi River, the Zambezi River in Africa, the Tigris River in Iraq, and even the Peruvian Amazon, at a distance of more than 3,000 miles from the ocean. This shark also lives in several lakes (such as Lake Nicaragua and Lake Izabal in Central America). By now it should be clear that we are discussing such a broad variety of predators, both small and large, that referring to just "sharks" in general really means very little. It's as misleading as talking about dogs and meaning only German shepherds, or speaking only of cocker spaniels and Pekingese but not even hinting at the existence of dogs as large as Saint Bernards.

Sharks are perfect hunting machines. Contrary to popular belief, however, they are not like wolves in the sense that they usually do not attack in packs, but are instead solitary hunters. This is probably because sharks are very primitive animals. In other words, elaborate hunting strategies involving the participation of several individuals—such as with killer whales or dolphins—are rare among sharks.

In the "feeding frenzies" of sharks, for example, each shark acts on its own. This aspect of shark behavior is confirmed by

Left: Oceanic white tip (*Carcharhinus longimanus*).
Opposite: Manta rays (*Manta birostris*), also called devilrays and devilfish, are the largest of the rays, with widths up to 22 feet. The broad body of this manta reflects moonlight as it swims near the surface of waters full of plankton, near the island of Kona, Hawaii.

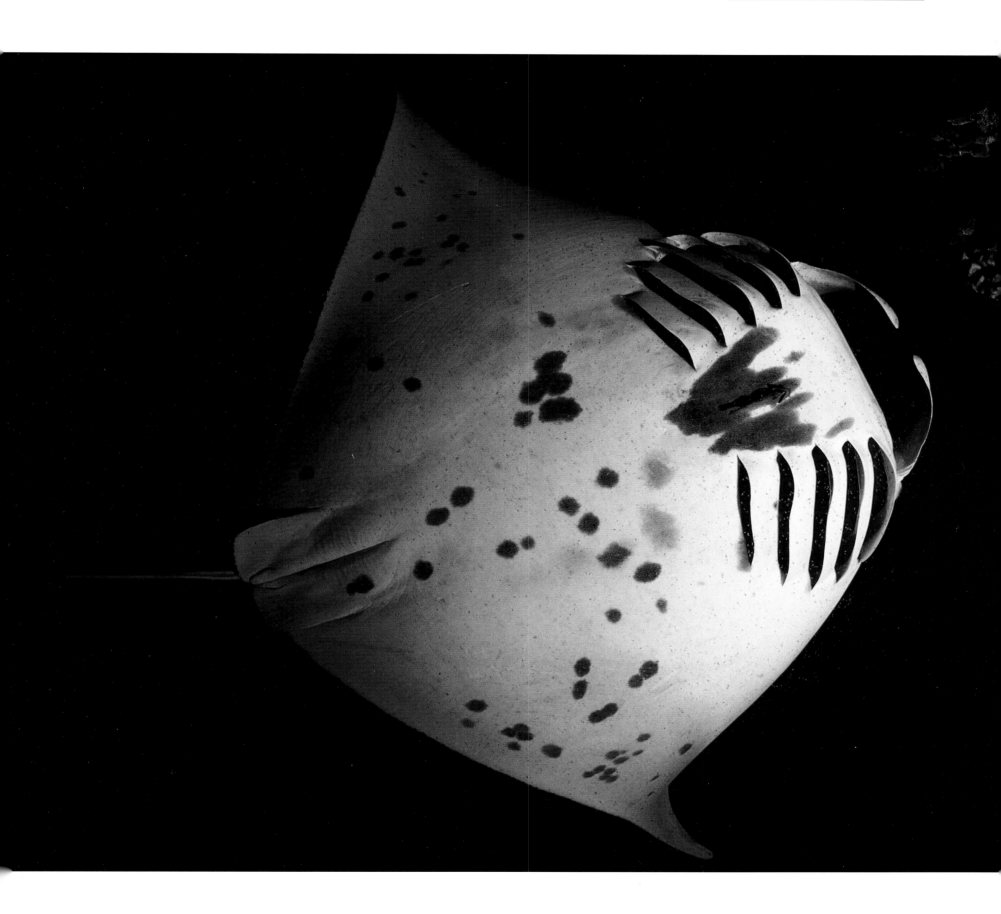

Left: Banjo shark (*Trygonorrhina sp. A*) photographed in Australian waters.

statistics of attacks on humans: more than 90 percent of the attacks involve a single shark. Some sharks, such as the Queensland shark (*Carcharhinus amblyrhynchoides*), let intruders know immediately when they have entered their territory. They arch their backs, make distorted swimming movements, wag their heads, point their pectoral fins downward, and swim in quick little bursts. If the intruder fails to understand such warning displays and comes closer, these sharks do not hesitate to attack. Many sharks use this kind of "display" behavior to send messages, so in a certain sense they communicate: this a new field that scientists have begun to explore only very recently.

During this century, humans have "invaded" more and more of the territory of sharks. Given the millions of divers, swimmers, fishermen, and others who enter or move across the water every year, the fact that there are occasional attacks should not be surprising. On the contrary, all things considered, the number of attacks seems small. It's a little like going for a picnic on the Serengeti Plain in Tanzania—no one would be too surprised if such a picnic ended with the intrusion of lions, rather than the usual ants. By attacking, sharks and lions are only exhibiting natural behavior, even if the prey, such as a human, is something not usually on their "menu." Predicting when or where a shark

will attack is not easy. There are some areas where a shark attack is more probable: certain stretches of coastline off South Africa, Australia, and California have the greatest number of attacks. But there is no definite place or time when an attack is more likely to happen. It can happen anywhere and at any time. Even so, several studies in the past have indicated that, statistically speaking, attacks tend to increase when the temperature of the water is over 68° F; they often take place during the hours between ten in the morning and noon, and then between two and six in the afternoon (with a peak at around three-thirty); they are most common when the sea is calm; and, finally, they take place

most often on Saturday and Sunday. It should be clear that these "preferred conditions" for an attack are the result of human preferences, not those of sharks. In other words, attacks happen where and when someone is swimming, and when someone goes swimming: it is likely that the water will be warm, not too cold; it will probably not be around meal times or when the water is choppy; and what better time to take a swim than the weekend? Furthermore, it's only logical that the greater the number of swimmers or divers active along a given stretch of coastline, the greater the possibility of an encounter with a shark, or even an attack. As a result, attacks are far more common in those countries where people are in the habit of going in the water: swimming, surfing, or playing some other aquatic sport. Which explains why analysis of the data from the American International Shark Attack File (the detailed record of all cases of shark attacks in all the countries of the world, begun by Dr. H. David Baldridge and today continued by Dr. George Burgess) reveals that two-thirds of the total number of attacks worldwide take place in the United States, Australia, South Africa, and the islands of the Pacific.

People often want to know if some particular behavior will put them at increased risk. Scuba divers hunting fish, who

Right: Whale shark (*Rhincodon typus*). When this shark senses danger, it tends to turn slowly, presenting its back (which is more heavily "armored") to the perceived threat. When a whale shark meets another shark, it may point its fins downward, thus making its body appear larger than it really is.

hang their bloody catch from their belts or attach it to floats nearby, stand an increased chance of a shark attack, particularly in tropical waters. That is only logical, but other interesting facts also emerge from the International Shark Attack File. Putting aside the type of coastline, water temperature, time of day, and so on, it emerges that almost two-thirds of attacks take place in water less than five feet deep and within fifty feet of the shore. Once again, this is clearly a result of human activity: 80 to 90 percent of swimmers are usually concentrated in the shallow water near the shore. This fact also reflects what many witnesses to a shark attack affirm: that there is no such thing as a "safety depth." Sharks attack everywhere, right up to the shore, even thrashing around in a few inches of water (although this is very rare). Generally, however, sharks prefer deep water and usually approach shorelines only at night. Oddly enough, in their attacks sharks show a marked preference for males over females (the ratio is 12 to 1). Perhaps this is simply because more men than women are involved in aquatic activities like deep-sea diving and underwater fishing.

"White death"

Often more than twenty feet long, the great white shark (*Carcharodon carcharias*) can weigh as much as a rhinoceros. One of the most dangerous predators in the ocean, it is known in Australia as "white death." As a peerless hunter, it depends on speed and surprise, and in that sense evolution has made it highly efficient. Unlike most cold-blooded fish and sharks, the great white is able to maintain a body temperature of up to 10 degrees above the temperature of the surrounding water; at that temperature its muscles work better.

The teeth of the great white shark (*Carcharodon carcharias*) are so symmetrical that Native Americans along the Florida coast once used them as arrowheads: they are triangular and have serrated edges that make them extremely sharp. As with almost all sharks, behind the first row of teeth stand another seven rows, ready to replace any lost teeth. It has been calculated that a shark will use, lose, and replace thousands of teeth over the course of its life (which lasts about 30 to 40 years). Many sharks swim in wide circles around their prey before making their first attack. In this way they "size up" the prey from a distance, using their chemical receptors to figure out what it is and then study its moves. This is not true of the white shark, which employs a completely different attack strategy. Used to attacking agile, fast-moving prey (sea lions, elephant seals, large fish, dolphins, and other sharks), it appears suddenly, moving at high speed like a torpedo. If the prey is swimming near the surface, the overwhelming attack comes from below. It tries to limit all contact with its prey at this point: the first attack is designed to deliver a strong enough bite

Above and right: The great white shark (*Carcharodon carcharias*). The gills of sharks, unlike those of other fish, are mobile and can contract or dilate according to need.

Left and opposite: Great white sharks (*Carcharodon carcharias*). Like makos (*Isurus oxyrinchus*), these sharks need increased respiration to make possible their sudden bursts of speed. For this reason their gills are longer and deeper than those of other, slower sharks.

charias), tiger sharks (*Galeocerdo cuvier*), and bull sharks (*Carcharhinus leucas*). One recent attack by a white shark took place in the Mediterranean Sea. The attack occurred about 20 yards from shore, and the victim got away safely, but not without suffering a terrible fright. She was paddling in a kayak when suddenly a shark about 11 feet long knocked her into the water. In all probability, the shark mistook the kayak for an animal (a marine mammal or large fish) and unleashed a classic attack from below. After taking three bites from the kayak, the shark realized its error and moved off. This saved the woman, who was almost immediately picked up by a small boat nearby. Dozens of witnesses on the beach saw the shark, which stayed in the area a short time before disappearing. The marks of the bites on the kayak (impounded by the authorities) were clearly visible, along with several embedded fragments of teeth.

Fatal attacks by white sharks (*Carcharodon carcharias*) are rare. For example, in this century only seven people are believed

that the victim will be rendered defenseless.

To protect its eyes from blows and scratches, the shark rolls its eyes back (rather like the headlights of a sports car) at the moment of the attack. It then swims off and waits at a safe distance for the victim to die from loss of blood. This same strategy is used in its attacks on humans.

The great white shark (*Carcharodon carcharias*), the only shark to truly merit the nickname "man-eater," can be found just about everywhere. One of the most peripatetic of all sharks, it rarely stays in one place for long, and makes long northward migrations in the warm months.

When white sharks (*Carcharodon carcharias*) attack humans, the attack is likely to be deadly. The International Shark Attack File attributes the most dangerous types of attacks, "bump and bite" and "sneak" attacks, to white sharks (*Carcharodon car-*

to have been killed by these sharks, far fewer than the number of people who have died as a result of bee stings. In the past, however, many attacks probably went unrecorded. After all, white sharks (*Carcharodon carcharias*) have inhabited the seas for millions of years, long before the first prehistoric humans arrived on the scene. Evidence of ancient shark attacks does exist, however, and it often turns up in the most unexpected places, such as Salsomaggiore, a landlocked city in northern Italy on the Po River. Throughout prehistory, all of the Po River region was beneath a shallow sea. Numerous fossilized white shark teeth have been found in the nearby countryside, along with the ribs of large prehistoric dolphins scarred with deep furrows caused by the teeth of white sharks. In one instance, the complete skeleton of a prehistoric cetacean was lifted out of sediment, and it too shows marks from the bites of a white shark (*Carcharodon carcharias*). Stuck in the ribs of this ancient marine mammal, and still plainly visible today, are two white shark teeth. In this region, so different today from the way it was 3-4 million years ago, the white shark commonly attacked and killed its victims.

Anatomy of a murderer

Whenever the subject of sharks comes up, sooner or later someone is sure to ask one particular question—Are sharks "intelligent" beings or are they no more than flesh-and-cartilage automatons ruled by their instincts? Of course, the question can't be answered without first establishing the meaning of intelligence. Is it the ability to learn? Or is it the ability to adapt to new conditions? No one today can provide a satisfactory answer to this question in terms of any living thing, sharks included. The fact remains that even though sharks are far more primitive than the bony fishes, they have on average a larger brain. This is partly a result of the fact that they are predators, and the areas of the brain related to the sense of smell, for example, are hyperdeveloped. Thanks to this notably superior "cerebral power," sharks are able to engage in relatively complex behavior.

- **What is a shark?**
- **An oversize liver**
- **Jet or pump-action?**
- **Hydrodynamics**
- **Turbo**
- **A swimming mouth**
- **From egg to umbilicus**

What is a shark?

Living in water means adapting to the rules of a three-dimensional world, a world denser than ours, airless and with less light. In adapting to the requirements of this environment, sharks have evolved a wide variety of behaviors: some remain suspended in the water, some hide on the bottom; some swim, others remain still; some depend on speed, others don't; some travel long distances, others are stationary. For these reasons, the various types of shark differ enormously one from another, with behaviors and biological adaptations that vary from species to species, from shark to shark.

Sharks are among the oldest vertebrates. Their group, and thus also their anatomy, has existed for nearly a half billion years, and over all that span of time sharks have changed hardly at all. From the point of view of taxonomy, sharks belong to the class of the cartilaginous fish, meaning their body contains no bones: the skull, the vertebrae, and the rays of the fins are made of cartilage, although in some species it is more or less calcified (the bodies of sharks contain small quantities of a tissue similar to bone that forms the basis

for their teeth). The cartilaginous fish are divided in two subclasses: the *Holocephali* (chimeras and related fish, 31 species) and the *Elasmobranchii* (sharks, rays, and skates, around 1,000 species). Aside from having no bones, sharks display various other interesting particularities. For example, they have no swim bladder, fertilization is always internal, and their skin is studded with tiny, toothlike structures called denticles. Sharks are found in all the seas and oceans of the world except for the Antarctic, where

they have never been spotted or captured.

Preceding pages, left: The fearsome snout of a sand tiger (*Eugomphodus taurus*).
Preceding pages, right: The snout of a lemon shark (*Negaprion breviostris*).

Above: A carpet shark (*Orectolobus ornatus*), or wobbegong, waits motionless, using its camouflage to blend in with the bottom; at the first opportunity, it will unleash a lightning attack, grasping its prey with its fanglike teeth.
Right: The Caribbean reef shark (*Carcharhinus perezi*), which can reach ten feet in length, is the most common shark in the Bahamas and the Gulf of Mexico. It is not unusual to find them seemingly napping on the sea bottom.

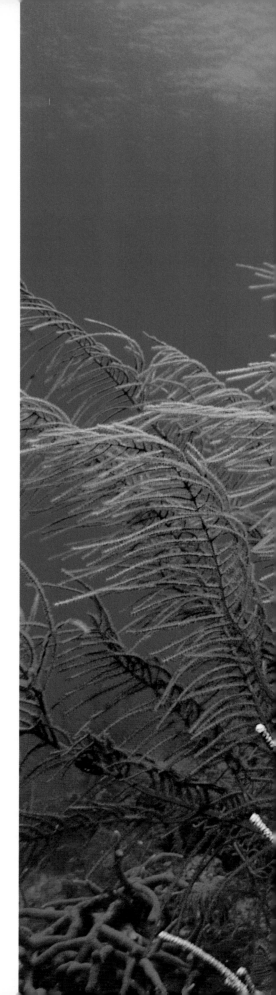

An oversize liver

Bony fish, meaning all fish with bony skeletons, have a swim bladder, a thin-walled sac full of gas that helps the fish float even if they do not move their fins. It also lets them move directly up or down simply by inflating or deflating the bladder, which functions something like an underwater life vest. A swim bladder is relatively slow in operation, however, and would be a terrible encumbrance in a lightning attack.

Left: The steady, black eye of a white shark (*Carcharodon carcharias*) is as big as a tennis ball. The experience of coming eye to eye with this shark is not soon forgotten.
Above: The blue-spotted bamboo shark (*Chiloscyllium caerulopunctatum*) is a bottom-dweller that reaches three feet in length.

Fish move quickly horizontally, but not vertically. A grouper, for example, can shoot off to the side, but is slow in moving straight up or down: it must synchronize with the pressure in its bladder, which inflates and deflates relatively slowly. If it failed to do so, it would explode or implode, which is what happens to many fish when they are caught and pulled quickly out of the water onto a fishing boat, and the bladder comes out of their mouths. In tuna, the swim bladder has nearly atrophied, which is why tuna move quickly in all directions. Sharks, however, have no swim bladder at all and can therefore take off in any direction the instant they spot prey, since they have nothing to inflate or deflate. Their attack capabilities are thus greater than with other fish—but without a bladder, how do they float? That problem has been solved in two ways: with a cartilaginous structure and with a very large liver.

In order to breathe and stay afloat, most sharks keep moving constantly, keeping the "motor" always running. Were their bodies any heavier,

they'd have to use up an enormous amount of energy just to stay afloat, but evolution has found a way around this problem. In place of a rigid, heavy skeleton, sharks have a skeleton made of much lighter cartilage. Cartilage is lighter than bone, but it's still heavier than water, so, in theory, sharks would still be too heavy to float: a little like us, in fact, since we can float only with our lungs full of air (a kind of makeshift swim bladder).

Evolution, however, has led to the development of another factor: a very large liver full of substances that float, lipids and squalene. This internal flotation system has adapted to suit the habits of the various species of shark. Sharks that swim near the surface cannot be too heavy, and in such sharks the liver can compose as much as 40 percent of the animal's entire body, thus reducing its terrestrial weight 40 times. This would be similar to a man weighing 175 pounds entering the water and instantly losing 170. This is why large sharks that are pulled out of the water sometimes die, crushed by their own body weight: the organs, without the support of a rigid rib cage, press together and are crushed. Sharks that live on ocean bottoms have smaller livers. If this were not the case, a strong current might lift them and carry them away.

The sand shark (*Eugomphodus taurus*) has a different system. If it wants to become lighter, it

rises to the surface and takes a deep breath of air—doing so makes it absolutely neutral and thus able to remain motionless in the water. When fishermen haul their line up and see air bubbles rising from the water, they know they've caught a sand shark—either that or a diver.

Opposite: A whale shark (*Rhincodon typus*) rises to the surface, where plankton is more abundant.
Left: The white-tip reef shark (*Triaenodon obesus*) is the shark most often encountered in tropical waters.
Below: The raised eyes of a tropical ray (*Taeniura lymma*) give it 360-degree vision.

Jet or pump action?

Sharks do not sleep the way we do—our bodies relatively motionless, our eyes closed, our blood pressure, breathing, and heartbeats slowed. When sharks sleep, they swim more slowly than they do when awake, but they swim nonetheless. Sharks are nearly always swimming, day and night, throughout its life. Why? To breathe. Sharks have no lungs, and they breathe like fish, by taking water in through their mouths and then forcing it out through gills.

An exchange of gases takes place during this process: as the water is drawn over the gills it leaves behind oxygen, which is carried into gill capillaries and thus into the shark's blood; at the same time the water takes away carbon dioxide. This "jet" type of respiration requires a constantly open mouth and continuous movement; put simply, the shark's forward motion pushes water into its mouth and then back out through its gills. This, the most common marine form of respiration, is found in all oceangoing sharks. Seemingly awkward, it has the advantage of making double use of the energy expended in swimming: it uses it to move and also to breathe. Some sharks take this process even further by adding other activities. Plankton-eating sharks like the whale shark (*Rhincodon typus*) move forward, breathe, and eat all at the same time, and always with their mouth open (to make this work even better this shark's mouth is located at the front of its head, rather than on the underside of its body). All sharks have gills, usually five, except for some primitive species that have six or even seven. Unlike the gills of other fish, shark gills are exposed and have no protective membrane. They are also mobile, which lets them contract or expand according to need. White sharks (*Carcharodon carcharias*) and mako sharks (*Isurus oxyrinchus*), which make

Above: The large spiracle of a small eagle ray (*Myliobatis sp.*) is clearly visible behind its eye.
Right: The unmistakable outline of a large whale shark (*Rhincodon typus*) swimming slowing along the bottom.

high-speed attacks, have larger respiratory needs, so their gills are longer and wider than those of other, slower-moving sharks.

Sharks like the carpet shark (*Orectolobus ornatus*), however, that remain relatively motionless on the bottom and do little swimming, don't suffocate. They breathe in a different way, using "pump action." Opening and closing their mouths contracts muscles that activate a kind of valve in their throats that breathes in water even if the shark is motionless using a system called branchial respiration. There is even a third method of respiration, that of the rays, in which water is taken in through two respiratory openings behind the eyes, known as spiracles. These holes have a valve activated by an involuntary muscle. All sharks have spiracles, but in many it is only an "optional," used to provide increased air to the brain. In the "modern" sharks, the spiracles are so small as to be almost invisible.

The sand shark (*Eugomphodus taurus*) is equipped for all means of respiration in the sense that, according to need, it can go from one to the other means of respiration. It uses the "pump-action" method while resting, and the "jet" when on the hunt.

Left: The gill slits of the whale shark (*Rhincodon typus*) are nearly a yard long and let in gallons of water each second.

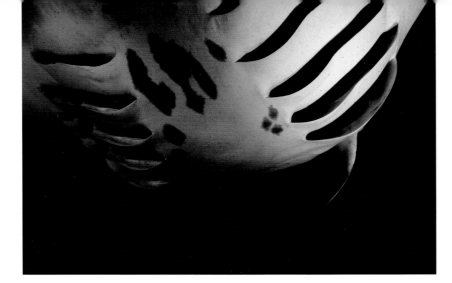

Above: Even manta rays (*Manta birostris*), like almost all sharks, have five gills.
Right: The Tasmanian seven-gill shark (*Notorhynchus cepedianus*) can reach more than ten feet in length.
Below: The large, maneuverable gill openings of the white shark (*Carcharodon carcharias*) provide rapid energy exchange, invaluable in acceleration and attacks. When more energy is needed, the gills contract to filter more water and thus furnish more oxygen to the body.

Hydrodynamics

A shark can be as long as a pencil—or as a bus. A shark can weigh a few ounces or a great many tons. There are sharks that live in the bright waters near the surface, and others that live only in the darkest depths of the abyss. Some cross entire oceans, others spend their lives lazily crisscrossing the waters of a reef. The variety seems infinite, but despite the myth, most sharks—80 percent—are less than six feet long, and more than half of them are best measured in inches.

As though following some adage about "never changing a winning combination," sharks have changed very little in terms of their overall design since they first came into being. They have, however, evolved into numerous types that are sometimes quite distinct from one another. There are various types for various purposes, such as to swim differently or to hunt different prey.

Some varieties of fish, such as dolphins, can be recognized immediately by some trait, in particular their way of swimming. Sharks share no such common trait, and they certainly don't all swim in the same way. Even so, the ways sharks swim can generally be divided into two basic types, one that can be called "eel" style and the other "tuna" style. The first style, in which the shark twists its body as does an eel, is slow, sinuous, and reflexive. The entire body snakes ahead, the head moving rythmically from right to left, with the forward drive provided by the hind areas of the body. This style of swimming makes it possible to cover great distances, but at no great speed. In search of food, the animal may be forced to perform migrations, even making long-distance oceanic voyages. Two blue sharks (*Prionace glauca*) tagged in New York were caught again several months later, one off the coast of Spain and the other off the coast of Brazil. This shark, considered a true ocean-trotter, can cover 30 miles a day and can swim at depths of more than 1,500 feet.

Sharks that swim using the "tuna" style are those that need speed to eat. These are not the sharks that eat small fish or squid, but those that chase fast-moving prey like bluefish, tuna, swordfish, or marlin. For these sharks the back-and-forth sweeping movements of the tail provide drive, while the rest of

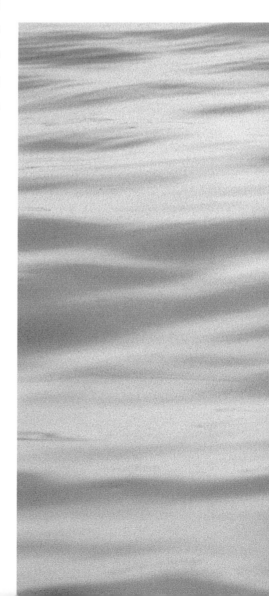

Opposite: Its tapered snout allows the white shark (*Carcharodon carcharias*) to glide through water like an immense, silent torpedo.

Left: The beak, or "prow," of a dolphin helps it cut through water. Thanks to its warm blood, streamlined body, and powerful swimming, dolphins are faster than sharks and have more endurance.

Below: A source of fear to swimmers the world over: a dorsal fin breaking the surface.

the body remains still. This way of swimming is more compact, but also far more vigorous and explosive.

Many sharks make use of both swimming techniques, changing from one to the other as they age: "eel"-style when young, "tuna" when fully grown. Almost all pelagic sharks, meaning those that live on the open

Left: The cartilaginous structure of a blue shark (*Prionace glauca*) is elastic and flexible, permitting it to bend itself almost into a U-shape, something usually impossible for a fish. *Below:* The pectoral fins of a manta ray (*Manta birostris*) form winglike appendages that make it look like it's flying when it swims.

seas, change their swimming style with age, with the exception of the white shark (*Carcharodon carcharias*), which swims the same way throughout its life.

The body sections of a shark, like the sections of a racing-yacht's hull, are not at all accidental in design and serve precise functions. They serve to increase maneuverability or speed, lift or acceleration, or they may help reduce "roll" or "pitch."

If we were to cut a shark in vertical slices down the length of its body, the slices would be of differing diameters, of course, but also of different shapes. We'd find ourselves with circles, ellipses, triangles, and polygons,

all of these different forms serving different functions. There would be nothing shaped like a ship's keel, however, since a shape like that would sink a shark. The tail, which is the motor and also the steering wheel, is vertical and sweeps horizontally, unlike the tail of whales, for instance, which are horizontal and move up and down, much like the flippers of a scuba diver. The tips of the tail (the lobes) move water like the oars of a ship. Differences in the shapes of these lobes result in differences in the kinds of propulsion.

In many sharks the upper lobe is more highly developed, and in

such cases, the "upper oar" tends to direct the animal downward. To compensate for this downward push, some sharks, such as the whale shark (*Rhincodon typus*) and hammerhead (*Sphyrina zygaena*), have broad, flattened heads; others, such as the thresher (*Alopias vulpinus*), have long pectoral fins. Such fins serve somewhat as stabilizers and somewhat as a kind of rudder. The dorsal fin, in particular, helps the shark maintain balance and keeps it from rolling over in the water. Pectoral fins provide lift, much like the wings of an airplane, and also brake forward movement. For this reason, swimming with large pectoral fins slows forward movement; it is something like swimming with the emergency brake on. Thanks to its large head and small pectoral fins, the hammerhead shark (*Sphyrina zygaena*) is a far faster swimmer than the thresher (*Alopias vulpinus*). The fins of the white shark (*Carcharodon carcharias*) are small in proportion to its body, but it is no racer: its cruising speed is about 3 miles an hour. At that speed it measures out its energy to preserve power for its attack, for otherwise it would be forced to eat constantly.

Bursts of lightning speed are

Right and opposite: Whale sharks (*Rhincodon typus*) can reach lengths up to 50 feet and weights of several tons. The shark's movement nearby causes a sudden displacement of water that divers can sense on their body and face mask.

usually an important attribute for a predator; the cheetah is an outstanding example. Such bursts are far more useful than the long-distance speed of a greyhound, which is good for covering ground but not for hunting. In water, an increase in size means an increase in speed with a diminished expenditure of energy. The larger an animal

Left: The fins of the white shark (*Carcharodon carcharias*) are comparatively short and aerodynamic. Their shorter size cuts down on the "drag" larger fins would create against water, and therefore do not impede the bursts of speed this predator needs to catch such fast-moving prey as tuna and seals.

Above: The head of a whale shark (*Rhincodon typus*) is broad, almost flat and blunt, with a long, straight mouth. The shark's enormous size makes up for the small size of its fins, which alone could not provide the lift needed to raise its head.

is, the faster it is. This is because the muscle mass is proportional to its volume, while the braking surface, and thus friction, is not. The body encounters less resistance and moves more quickly; just like a ship.

Above: At depths of nearly 100 feet in the waters off La Paz, Baja California, one can find large groups of hammer-head sharks (*Sphyrna lewini*). Getting near these sharks is not easy, for they are shy and skittish, dislike noises, and flee as soon as they spot a diver's air bubbles. Divers must either do without

air tanks or hold their breath, both of which are difficult and dangerous. *Opposite:* Like the keel of an over-turned sailboat, the large dorsal fin stabilizes the "hull" of a whale shark (*Rhincodon typus*). The pectoral fins are small and arched like the wings of a kite.

Following pages, left: The long tail fin of a whale shark (*Rhincodon typus*). *Following pages, right:* An oceanic white tip (*Carcharhinus longimanus*) with traveling companions.

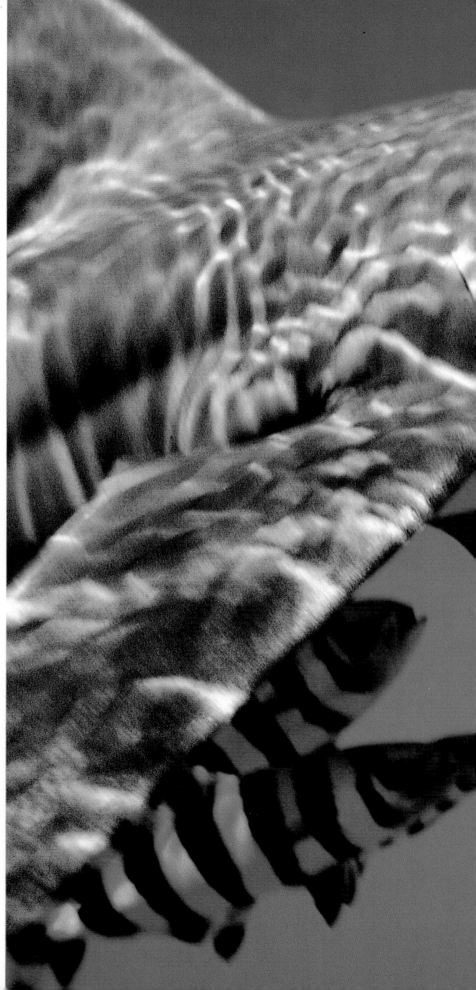

Turbo

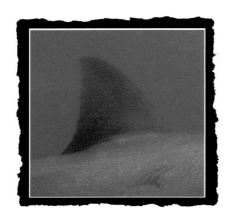

If we fed all the relevant data into a computer and had it design a high-seas racer, it would probably come up with a design with these characteristics: symmetrical tail for smooth propulsion; small pectoral fins to cut down on friction; rigid dorsal fin for stabilization; cylindrical body with grooves for smooth movement; pointed snout to better cut through the water; large gills to provide increased oxygen; and perhaps even warm blood to increase power and endurance. All in all, something along the lines of a torpedo—and such a being exists in nature: it's the mako shark.

The mako (*Isurus oxyrinchus*) is the only shark that leaps out of the water. It may perform such leaps to rid itself of parasites; the exact reason is unknown. It has been calculated that to make a leap of 15 feet it must reach a speed of over 22 miles an hour, and it seems capable of bursts up to 35 miles an hour. How do you measure the speed of a shark? First, you measure the speed of an ocean current. If a shark swimming against that current succeeds in

staying still, it means its speed is equal to that of the current.

This shark can travel as far as 40 miles a day in search of tuna. It can turn, stop, or accelerate quite suddenly, and has excellent maneuverability. The only thing it can't do is swim backward. But no shark can do that, although fish can. In most cases, the body of a shark maintains the same temperature as the surrounding water (they are ectotherms), but some adjust their temperature to their behavior. For example, the blue shark (*Prionace glauca*), after eating, rises to the surface in search of warm water in which to digest. The warm water accelerates all metabolic processes, including digestion and growth. Having finished digesting, the blue shark descends to cooler water to preserve energy and to avoid having to eat continuously. Like the white shark (*Carcharodon carcharias*) and the thresher (*Alopias vulpinus*), the mako (*Isurus oxyrinchus*) keeps its body temperature a few degrees higher than the surrounding water. Its "heater" is a band of muscle, full of tiny capillaries and packed with red corpuscles (the *rete mirabilia*). The blood thus reaches a larger surface, warming tissue, muscles, and the brain.

A machine that produces so much heat must also burn more fuel. The result is that digestion is faster, and the shark's appetite is increased.

Preceding pages and right: These photographs of a mako (*Isurus oxyrinchus*) were taken during a single brief encounter off the coast of San Diego, California. A shape appeared in the blue—the mako—and all at once it attacked. The attack came with lightning speed: one swift bite crushed the flash attachment, the electrical circuits of which must have interfered with the shark's sense organs, attracting its interest.

Unlike other pelagic sharks such as the blue shark (*Prionace glauca*), the mako (*Isurus oxyrinchus*) does not swim in circles around its prey, does not "sample" it with its "on-board chemical laboratory": it bites and that's it. This shark's diet changes as it ages. As an embryo it eats the unfertilized eggs that its mother produces. When first born it eats squid; but once fully grown, with its tapering teeth curved like claws, it tears into deep-sea fish. It shows a preference for bluefish, which it swallows whole.

A swimming mouth

Sharks are true "swimming mouths." Not because they're voracious, but because of the way they attack prey. Their skin is covered with small papillae called "pit organs" that test the water and sense the composition of objects that touch their victims, before the final attack. Thus, the body of a shark is a kind of "tongue," and it is a tongue furnished with a set of teeth. These "teeth" are the small, toothlike structures known as denticles that stud the shark's body.

The skin of sharks is so rough that it has been used as a kind of sandpaper, called "shagreen," and it also provides sharkskin, a durable leather. The skin of every shark species has a different kind of denticle,

Above: The gaping jaws of a lemon shark (*Negaprion brevirostris*).
Right: The tiger shark (*Galeocerdo cuvier*), one of the most dangerous.
Far right: A blue shark (*Prionace glauca*) breaks the surface while chasing prey. The protective membrane that covers the eyeball is highly visible.

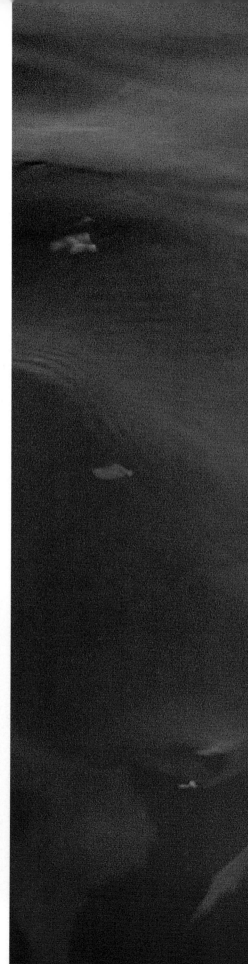

Left: A blue shark (*Prionace glauca*) swims closer to examine a diver. *Above:* A whale shark (*Rhincodon typus*) feeding on the high seas.

Following pages: This blue shark (*Prionace glauca*), off the coast of San Diego, seems to be standing still to pose for the camera. What seems like a tranquil moment was actually potentially dangerous because of the strong current (the diver on the left is tied to a boat on the surface to avoid being swept away).

but they are all very much like tiny teeth. The faster the shark, the smaller the denticles. The skin of sharks has other interesting characteristics. It has a "grain" and a "countergrain," according to the direction of movement. Also, the denticles permit the efficient passage of water, which moves between

one scale and another, creating a kind of "damper" that lets the shark silently "stalk" prey, much as a lion will approach a gazelle from downwind.

How do sharks bite their prey? In most sharks, the mouth is located on the underside of the body, well behind the long snout. In antiquity, people

believed that sharks had to roll onto their backs in order to bite their prey.

In reality, the jaws of a shark are about the most efficient that nature has designed for a predator. The upper jaw is not fused to the skull, as it is in lions or humans, instead it is connected at only a few points, making it highly mobile. In effect, the upper jaw is "loose"

and, together with the lower jaw (the mandible), they form a kind of trap lined with teeth. Just before biting, the shark spreads open this trap and lifts its snout so that all the victim sees is the gaping mouth of some unknown enemy. It sees a long dark tunnel with an entrance studded by sharp teeth. The shark most certainly does not roll onto its back.

Sharks have no molars and cannot move their jaws sideways: they swallow prey without chewing. Often, however, sharks bite up their prey or cut it into large pieces (for example, if biting the carcass of a dolphin). Watching a shark bite is a memorable experience. To cut through the skin of its prey a shark may shake its head violently from side to side, much

Above and opposite: A small lemon shark (*Negaprion brevirostris*) and, in particular, its teeth. As small as it is— about a yard long—this shark could cut through a human leg with a single bite.

like a dog; in doing so, it makes it jaws into "saws" that can rip through skin and muscles in an instant.

Take a close look at the jaws of a shark: behind each tooth there are several more rows of teeth (usually seven). These are "extra" teeth ready to replace lost teeth. Sharks damage and easily lose teeth during their attacks because, unlike human teeth, their teeth have no roots and are simply "glued" to the jaws with a wide base set only slightly in the cartilage.

When a tooth is lost, another soon comes forward to replace it; another then begins growing at the end of the row. In the instant of biting, some sharks, such as the white shark (*Carcharodon carcharias*), roll their eyes back to protect them from the desperate thrashing of the victim; others, such as the blue shark (*Prionace glauca*), use a protective "eyelid."

One of the most singular

Opposite: At about 40 feet in length, a whale shark (*Rhincodon typus*) looms in the water like a city bus. Although the shark is harmless, divers can't help experiencing a touch of fear near its gaping mouth: it might suck someone in purely by accident.
Above: This small tiger shark (*Galeocerdo cuvier*) was so aggressive it bit the lens opening in the camera case, forcing us to get out of the water.
Right: A whale shark (*Rhincodon typus*) closes its mouth only rarely and only for short periods.

aspects of shark biology is that every species—and there are more than 370—has teeth of a different shape: some cut, others lacerate, some saw, others grind. There are also those sharks that are almost toothless; rather than bite, they suck.

Actually, teeth can be used to identify a species of shark much as if they were a kind of fingerprint. In some cases just a single tooth is enough to identify a shark, while in other cases

The series of photographs on these pages shows a great white shark (*Carcharodon carcharias*) approaching and attacking the carcass of a tuna on the surface. The shark seems to understand that the prey won't flee; the caution it demonstrates in the attack may be caused by the unusual situation and, perhaps, by the large red buoy to which the carcass is tied. One can clearly see that the shark opens its jaws even while still more than ten feet away from its prey. During the last moments of the attack the shark can no longer see, having rolled back its eyes to protect them, but the attack is not blind: during the final instants the attack is guided by the shark's ampullae of Lorenzini.

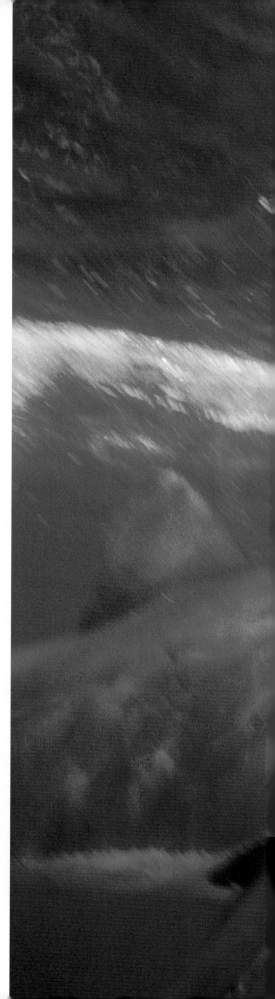

just a section of skin will do the trick.

Yes, the skin, for the teeth of sharks are a part of their skin, not their skeleton (as with fish), and they are constantly being reproduced.

Replacement teeth are always slightly larger than the ones they replace. The Caribbean reef shark (*Carcharhinus perezi*),

which has more than 300 teeth, uses about fifty at a time. In general, only the first and second rows are functional. The white shark (*Carcharodon carcharias*) has serrated teeth that are almost perfectly triangular. The white shark replaces its teeth one at a time every two or three weeks. It's worth adding that it loses up

to a dozen at every meal.

The teeth of makos (*Isurus oxyrinchus*) and sand sharks (*Eugomphodus taurus*) are long and pointed with slight hooks to grab and hold small fish and squid. The teeth of a tiger shark (*Galeocerdo cuvier*) are wide at the base and have an oblique, sharpened point to perforate the shells of turtles.

Above: The teeth of a triakid, in this case a gummy shark (*Mustelus antarcticus*). The upper jaw is a kind of rasp that, together with the mandible, can grind up small fish.
Opposite: What seems to be the face of a strange creature is actually the snout of a stingray (*Dasyatis sp.*). This side usually rests on the bottom. The holes that seem like eyes are actually nostrils; the eyes are on the other side of the head, facing upward. Visible in its mouth are its rows of teeth, which it uses to grind up invertebrates.

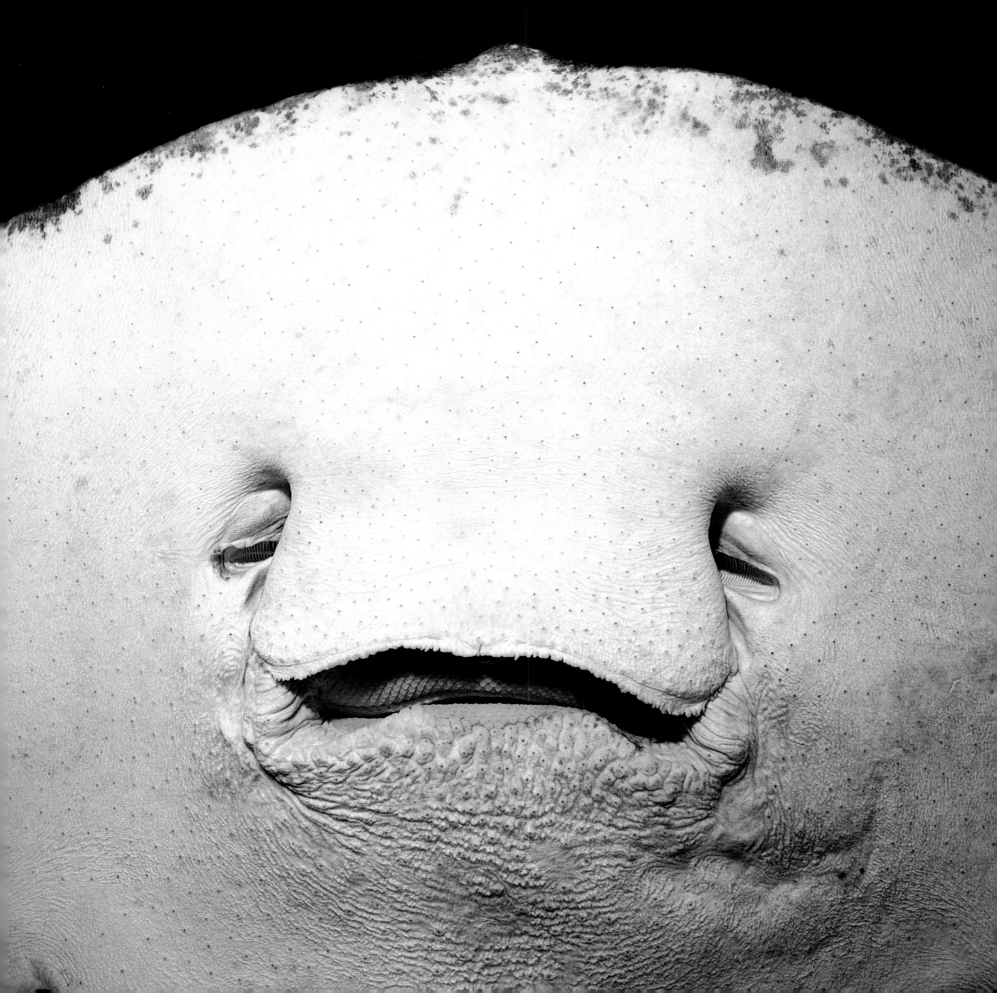

There are also the odd teeth of certain bottom-dwelling sharks, such as the smooth hound (*Mustelus mustelus*), a member of the triakid family of sharks, that usually grows to about 3 feet in length. The sharks in this family have small, rounded teeth set close together, each with several cusps, creating a kind of tooth mosaic that covers both jaws; the shark uses this like a nut-cracker to break the shells of crustaceans and mollusks. In these sharks the teeth are replaced in blocks, one row at a time.

Above: This jawbone covered with blunt, ridged, grinding teeth reflects the eating habits of its former owner, an eater of shellfish, urchins, and mollusks.

Right: A sand tiger (*Eugomphodus taurus*) with a remora attached to its throat. A glance at a shark's teeth will usually tell you what it eats. This one uses its sharp, curling teeth to grab small fish, cuttlefish, and squid. Shark teeth vary not only from species to species and with age, but in some cases even from male to female.

Opposite: The Port Jackson shark (*Heterodontus portusjacksoni*). Looking one of these sharks in the eyes is difficult, since its eyes are on the top of its head. But vision is not important to this shark, because it hunts at night. Its sense of smell, however, is invaluable, and this explains the two curling nostrils located at the sides of its mouth. The borders of the nostrils are exposed to present the greatest possible surface area to the water, resulting in a highly sensitive chemical detection device.

From egg to umbilicus

Why deny it? Courtship behavior among sharks lacks a certain finesse. Rather than using tender caresses to win over the female, the male relies instead on carefully aimed bites to her back, fins, and sides. It may not seem very gentlemanly, but it works. The female of the blue shark (*Prionace glauca*), bearing in mind the behavior of males, has developed certain countermeasures: her skin is three times thicker than that of her companion and, most importantly, thicker than the length of his teeth. Shark love bites serve not only to stimulate the female but also to hold her still during copulation. For all sharks copulate, just like human beings, and they began doing it millions of years earlier.

Small sharks mate clutching each other, sometimes twisted together; larger and heavier sharks mate side by

Left: The male sex organs (claspers) of a white shark (*Carcharodon carcharias*). The shark has two, but only one at a time is functional, the other being kept in reserve.
Above: The female genitals. The male fertilizes the female internally, in a mating process similar to that of mammals.

side, head to head and stomach to stomach. The male reproductive structure (clasper) penetrates the female organ (cloaca) and, to avoid falling out, attaches itself with a hook-shaped anchor. The sperm pass rapidly into the female from two large internal testes, together with a strong flow of sea water. If the female becomes agitated she may break a clasper. This is not a problem, for the male has

two, although only one functions at a time. The clasper continues growing throughout the life of the shark, as does the rest of its body, and it changes appearance with time. When the animal is young the claspers are short and soft; over the years they calcify and harden. Some sharks, such as the blue shark (*Prionace glauca*), hammerhead (*Sphyrina zygaena*), and sand shark (*Eugomphodus taurus*),

mate every year; other sharks every two years; still others year-round, with no fixed calendar. Ovulation usually follows several weeks after mating.

The blue shark (*Prionace glauca*) reaches sexual maturity at six years, but can mate at four. To avoid losing reproductive opportunities, which are important to any migratory animal, the female can store live sperm in her body for as long as two years. Do baby sharks grow inside the body of their mother or outside? That depends. The cat shark (*Cephaloscyllium ventriosum*) lays eggs just as a hen does. The blue shark (*Prionace glauca*) has a placenta similar to that in mammals, including humans. The baby white shark (*Carcharodon carcharias*) also grows inside the body of its mother, but inside a separate yolk sac without the nutritive substances of a placenta. About 30 percent of all sharks are oviparous, meaning they lay eggs; about 50 percent are viviparous and aplacental, meaning they produce eggs that open inside the body; and about

The egg case of a cat shark (*Cephaloscyllium ventriosum*). Those sharks that reproduce by depositing eggs are the most biologically ancient and the least developed. Highly visible in the case is the yolk that will provide nourishment to the embryo during the gestation period, which lasts about nine months.
Opposite: The blue shark (*Prionace glauca*) is the most prolific shark, giving birth on average to 40 young—but as many as 135 have been recorded.

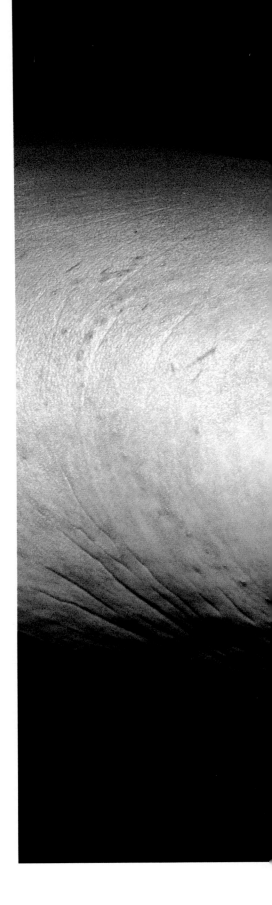

20 percent are viviparous and placental, meaning they create a primitive "placenta" to nourish the embryo.

The simplest reproductive method is to lay eggs and wait. This is the method used by birds, fish, reptiles, and amphibians. Of the many eggs that are laid, some are almost certain to survive environmental perils and the jaws of predators and grow into young members of the species. With sharks, the parents must expend only a modest amount of energy: they deposit the fibrous sac that contains the eggs in the rocky cracks of a reef or among the branches of a coraline growth. After 9 to 10 months the young will force their way through the walls of the sac and slip out: the newborn are small, but they're ready to bite. This system works for bottom-dwelling sharks that eat invertebrates. However on the open sea, where things change

rapidly and the newborn must be more fully equipped in order to find food and survive, development almost always takes place inside the body of the mother. For some months the embryo swims in the uterus and feeds off the yolk sac. When it finishes the contents of the sac, it devours the eggs that the mother's ovaries continue to produce. When embryos of the sand tiger (*Eugomphodus taurus*) finish eating these eggs, they

eat the other fertilized embryos. Usually only two embryos survive, one from each uterus (sharks have two separate uteri). After placental sharks have consumed the contents of the yolk sac, they receive uterine milk: a rich mixture that nourishes the embryo until the placenta is ready for it. When the placenta is fully formed, the source of nourishment improves since the embryo then receives food and oxygen directly. At the end of the gestation period, the females stop eating and use up the accumulated fats—a method whereby they resist the temptation to devour their young.

Shark "nurseries" are areas where females go to give birth to their young, and certain locations are associated with particular species. The blue shark (*Prionace glauca*), for example, has chosen certain areas of the Adriatic Sea as the ideal setting in which to give birth, making it the most common species in those waters. The area of the Mediterranean between Sicily and Tunisia is associated with the great white shark (*Carcharodon carcharias*), and local fishermen often catch young white sharks, mistaking them for young mako sharks (*Isurus oxyrinchus*).

Above: Horn shark. *Left:* The characteristic spiral egg case of a Horn shark.
Right: The sand tiger (*Eugomphodus taurus*) is the least prolific of all sharks.

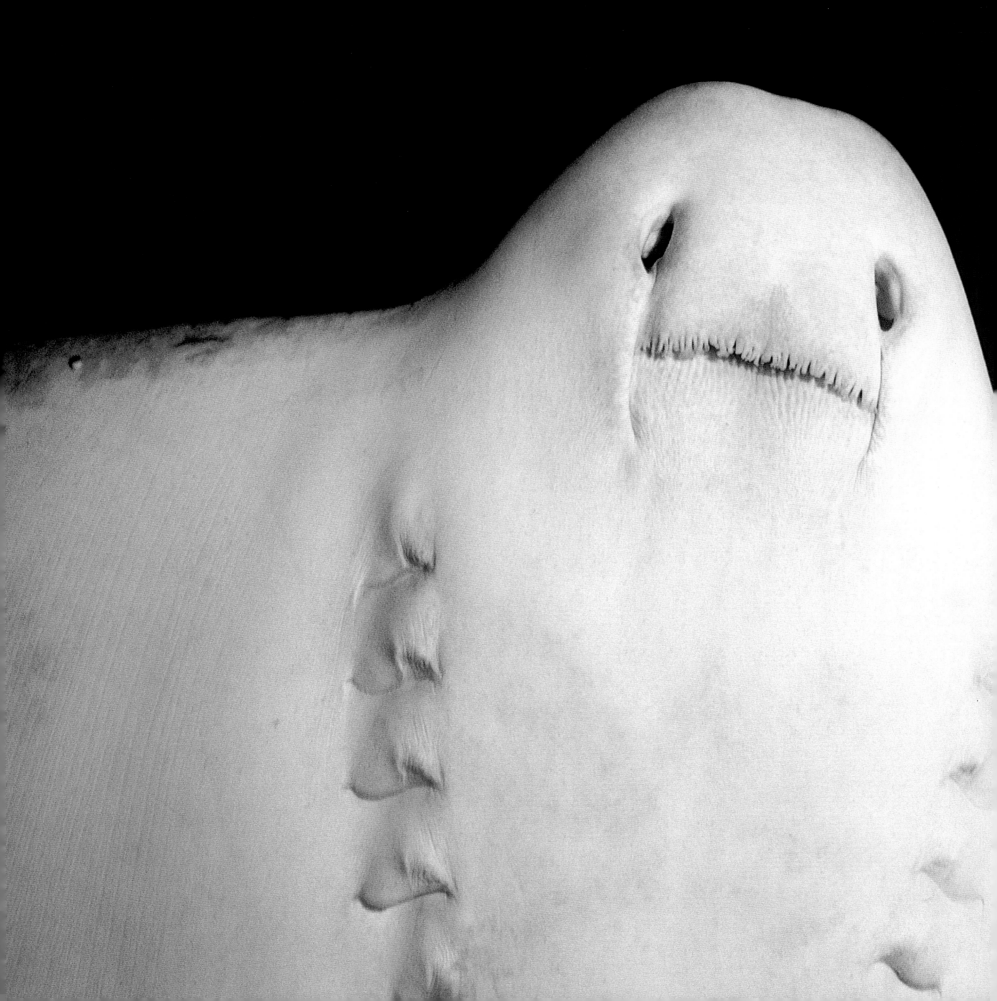

The seven senses

Sharks have the same senses as humans: touch, sight, smell, hearing, and taste. They also have two others that are unknown to us that we might call the sixth and seventh senses. The sixth is a kind of long-distance sense of touch. Thanks to two "lateral lines," one on each flank of the body, sharks can perceive the waves of pressure created by the body movements of their prey, even at a distance of hundreds of yards. The seventh sense is the ability to perceive electrical fields: using certain pores in the head area (the so-called ampullae of Lorenzini), sharks can make out the electric field of their prey, and they are guided by this "radar" during the final moments of their attack.

- **Long-distance sensing**
- **Shark eyes**
- **Electric smell**
- **The body tongue**

Long-distance sensing

Unlike our nostrils, the nostrils of sharks serve only to smell and not to breathe; with a few rare exceptions, such as the nurse shark (*Ginglymostoma cirratum*), the nostrils are not connected to the respiratory system. A shark's nostrils look like small, round chambers, and inside them is an olfactory membrane. To facilitate the entry of water, the edge of the nostril is folded in a particular way (the so-called folds of Schneider). These folds channel water that runs along the snout during swimming, creating a constant flow to the nostrils.

The sensitivity of sharks to chemical substances in water is astonishing: they can identify one part of blood in 100 million parts of water. Recent studies conducted by scientist Robert E. Hueter and Professor Perry W. Gilbert have concluded that gray reef sharks (*Carcharhinus amblyrhyncos*) and black-tipped reef sharks (*Carcharhinus melanopterus*) can identify a hunk of grouper skin in a concentration equal to one part in 10 billion. This would be like making out a drop of wine in the con-

tents of a small swimming pool. In hunting prey, the shark relies initially on smell. Having picked up an interesting chemical trace, the shark follows it, somewhat like a hound dog being drawn to the scent of game. The shark zigzags back and forth as it swims in pursuit, its snout swinging right and left, and its nostrils "sniffing" through great quantities of water. In this way the shark is able to lock on to the "scent trail" of its prey and follow it with enormous precision.

The sea has been called a

silent realm, but in truth it's full of noises. Sounds are easier to hear underwater because water is denser than air (750 times denser), and the denser the substance it must move through,

Preceding pages, left: An eagle ray.
Preceding pages, right: Silvertip shark (*Carcharhinus albimarginatus*), photographed in Papua New Guinea.

Above: The bamboo shark (*Chiloscyllium punctatum*) eats small fish and invertebrates.
Right: Unlike most other sharks, the nostrils of the nurse shark (*Ginglymostoma cirratum*) are connected to its respiratory system.

the faster sound travels. Which is why a sound travels five times faster in water than in the air and covers greater distances.

Sharks perceive sounds with their whole body, but it is pri-

Above: Sharks have a "third eye," similar to the pineal gland in vertebrates. In this lemon shark (*Negaprion brevirostris*), the organ is highly developed and receives luminous stimuli, thanks to a small opening in the cranium which permits the passage of light.

Left: Most carcharinids, like this one, eat only fish and cephalopods. They eat abundantly when they have the opportunity so as to better face long periods without food.

Right: Like horses on a carousel, these blue sharks (*Prionace glauca*) are swimming around a diver. This behavior is, however, anything but playful: the sharks are following their standard attack strategy, which begins by circling the prey.

marily the inner ear that makes out the exact source of a sound. The shark's inner ear is composed of two structures that are not outwardly visible except for two tiny pores located behind the eyes. They are highly sensitive to low-frequency sounds (under 100 Hertz) and to irregular vibrations, which they can identify from more than a mile away. Furthermore, because of otoliths (stony concretions) suspended in fluid in the inner ear, sharks can perceive gravity and are thus able to swim upright even at night or in the abyssal darkness. Sharks also have a "sixth sense," a sort of "long-distance touch," something like what happens when we feel a breeze on the hairs of a forearm, or when a car passes nearby and we feel the force of the air on our skin.

Shark eyes

Contrary to popular belief, sharks have excellent eyesight, and it is an eyesight well adapted to their marine environment. Even in the clearest water, it is impossible to see over miles of distance. Organic particles suspended in water absorb light and cloud the water, usually reducing visibility to a few dozen yards. What is needed, therefore, is not sharp vision, but vision that is highly sensitive to the scarce amount of luminosity. In this sense sharks are well equipped, for over the course of their evolution their corneas, pupils, lenses, and retinas have made suitable adaptations.

There are also many differences in eyesight among the various species. Some sharks that hunt both by day and by night have contractile pupils (similar to those of a cat) that adapt to available luminosity. Others, for example, the sharks that live at great depths where darkness is constant, have fixed, greatly dilated pupils. This permits them to make out the weak glow given off by their prey, which are often bioluminescent.

Almost all sharks can "see" at night because behind the retina they have a reflecting layer, or "mirror," the *tapetum lucidum*, which enhances vision and helps them see better in even the weakest light. During the day

Above: The eye of a ray covered by a strange trefoil lid.
Right: Detail of the slitlike pupil of the blue-spotted bamboo shark (*Chiloscyllium caerulopunctatum*).
Opposite: Almost all carcharhinids have circular eyes with no barbels on the nostrils.

this mirror is covered by a "veil" that keeps luminous rays from being reflected and thus protects the retina. Experiments performed on the retinas of sharks (to measure the number of particular nerve cells that perceive the differing wavelengths of colors) have determined that some sharks, such as the great white shark (*Carcharodon carcharias*), see in color, while others see only in black and white.

Opposite: Carpet shark (*Orectolobus ornatus*). The size of a shark's eyes indicates the importance of vision to its hunting methods. Unlike open-sea predators, sharks that live on sea floors have small eyes.
Right: The eyes of a whale shark (*Rhincodon typus*) are tiny in proportion to its body. Good vision, however, has nothing to do with capturing the microorganisms that constitute its diet.
Below: Like a curtain, the nictitating membrane protects the eyes of all carcharhinids. White sharks (*Carcharodon carcharias*) and makos (*Isurus oxyrinchus*), on the other hand, roll their eyes back so that they disappears.

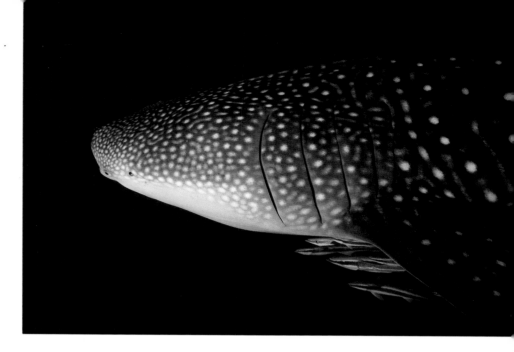

Electric smell

Almost half a billion years of evolution have gifted sharks with a sophisticated sense of electric fields. How does it work? In a certain sense, it works like the metal detectors used to locate metal objects on a person or land mines buried underground: in the final phase of an attack, the shark uses this system to direct the last yards of its movement so as to hit the prey directly. Every possible victim of a shark attack (including a human) creates a small electromagnetic field around itself that the shark can perceive with its detectors. Most of the "operators" in this communications system are concentrated in the shark's snout.

The so-called ampullae of Lorenzini (named for the Italian anatomist Stefano Lorenzini, who first described them in 1678) are a dense group of small pores and minuscule cavities filled with a gelatinous substance containing nerve cells sensitive to electric fields. This ingenious system permits sharks to not only perceive electric fields but also their intensity and direction. In this way a shark can follow prey in absolute darkness or detect it when hidden. Hammerhead sharks (*Sphyrina zygaena*), for example, can perceive the locations of rays hidden beneath sand. The ampullae of Lorenzini may also function as a sort of navigational compass, enabling the shark to perceive the earth's magnetic field, the variations around wreckage or underwater volcanic cones, even the currents running parallel to islands. Laboratory experiments have shown that some sharks can even make out variations of only 5 billionths of a volt per square centimeter—this is the highest electric sensitivity in all of the animal kingdom. At close distances, an electrical field is the most important stimulus for a shark, so much so that it can cause it to commit unusual errors: reportedly a white shark (*Carcharodon*

Left: Attracted by the camera, a blue shark (*Prionace glauca*) approaches to within a few inches of the lens. The shark is so close that three tiny parasites are clearly visible attached over its eye.
Above: Detail of the ampullae of Lorenzini, small pores in front of the nostrils.

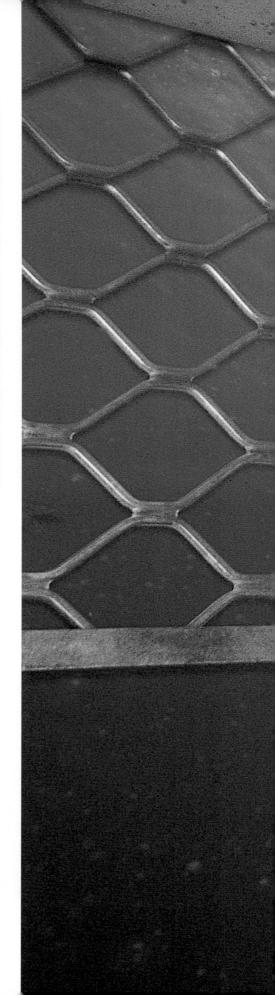

carcharias) attracted by a floating slice of bloody tuna suddenly veered off course and bit the bars of the metallic cage in which scuba divers had taken shelter. After giving the cage and its occupants a few furious shakes, the shark realized its error.

Above: Sharks swim and hunt as though they had compasses on the tips of their noses providing constant information on the ocean around them and helping them locate prey.
Right: The broad surface of the snout of a hammerhead (*Sphyrna lewini*) offers more space for the nerve center, thus permitting it to sniff out and locate rays, devilfish, and other prey even under the sand.
Opposite: The electromagnetic field generated by the metal cage has fooled a white shark (*Carcharodon carcharias*), which bites into and furiously shakes the cage.

The body tongue

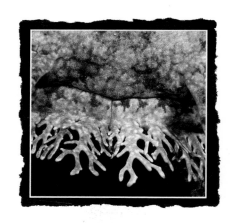

Sharks often give prey a little blow or just touch it with their snout before making their final attack. This behavior is comparable to reading the menu in a restaurant. In fact, tiny sensors, similar to the taste buds on our tongue, are spread along the surface of a shark's skin. By means of these, a shark tastes its prey before biting it. And that isn't all.

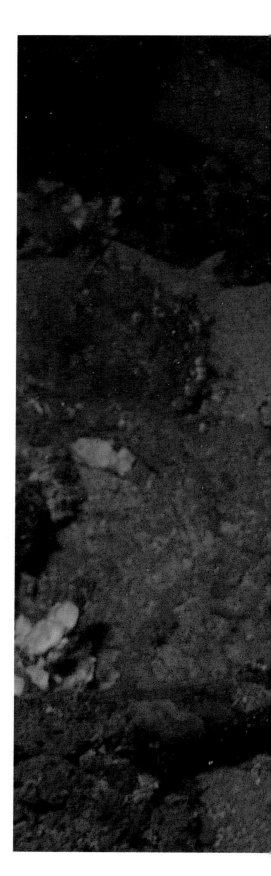

Above: Detail of the mouth of a carpet shark (*Orectolobus sp.*).
Left: A guitarfish, a ray with a shovel-shaped nose. Such rays are less than a yard in length and eat small crustaceans that move along the bottom.
Right: A carpet shark resembles a harmless drifting bush, but its enormous mouth is always ready to snatch any fish that comes close enough. The strange formations are not sensory organs but growths, known as dermal lobes or tassels, that improve its camouflage.

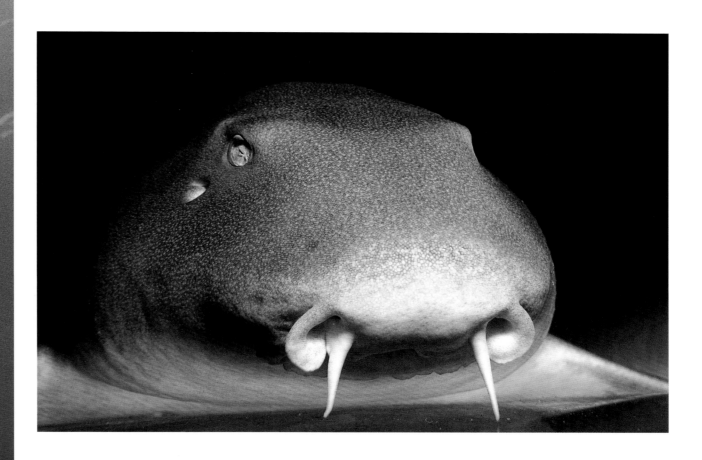

Left: As with alligators, the Achilles heel of a shark is its nose. This diver has immobilized a six-foot-long blue shark (*Prionace glauca*) using the palm of his hand. Turning the shark over so that its stomach is upward also helps to pacify it.

Above: In some sharks that live on the bottom the barbels are used to test prey.

Even as it bites, a shark continues to taste its victim using the papillae in its mouth, and if it doesn't like the taste, the victim is immediately spit out. This has happened many times in instances of white sharks (*Carcharodon carcharias*) attacking humans. It would seem that human flesh does not appear on the usual menu of sharks. After hundreds of millions of years of eating fish, crustaceans, turtles, marine birds, seals, and mollusks, human flesh, it seems, can be an unpleasant novelty. Which is why many sharks seem suspicious when they taste it. Unfortunately, not all sharks display such refined taste, and some, in fact, such as the tiger shark (*Galeocerdo cuvier*), gobble up absolutely anything, even metallic objects.

A genus of flatfish (or sole) that lives in the Red Sea and Indian Ocean, the Moses sole (*Pardachirus marmoratus*), exploits the taste sensitivity of white-tip reef sharks (*Triaenodon obesus*) to avoid being eaten by them. It emits a milky secretion containing a highly toxic substance called pardaxin, which reacts to the surface of shark gills. The result is that sharks make no attempt to bite it, no matter how hungry they get.

Prey

All sharks are carnivores. Some, however, such as the whale shark (*Rhincodon typus*) and basking shark (*Cetorhinus maximus*), are specialists at hunting tiny prey visible only under a microscope: these are the so-called "plankton," made up of microscopic algae (phytoplankton) and animals (zooplankton), along with an abundance of larvae and large quantities of small crustaceans that live in teeming masses. It is an abundant biomass, more numerous than all the world's fish put together, and, most importantly, enormously rich in lipids and proteins. Eating it is not simple, however; these sharks find themselves facing a giant bowl of rice in which the grains jump away in every direction. The solution is simple: swim along slowly with your mouth open wide.

- **Ambush on the high seas**
- **A stomach of iron**

Ambush on the high seas

Hunting calls for more than just a powerful body; it also requires a predator's skills. Just as lions on the savanna don't spend all day chasing around behind antelopes, sharks at sea, to avoid burning up their energy in useless charges and tiring swims, have to perfect hunting strategies to exploit surprise and turn to their advantage every error made by their prey; that is, if they don't want to end the day exhausted.

Preceding pages, left: Healthy adult sea lions and seals can outswim sharks. The element of surprise is necessary for a shark to successfully attack.
Preceding pages, right: Mackerel, bluefish, and tuna are the favorite prey of sharks like the mako (*Isurus oxyrinchus*), great white (*Carcharodon carcharias*), and thresher (*Alopias vulpinus*).

Above: An eagle ray.
Right: In Hawaii large rays can be spotted at night as they hunt for plankton by the light of the moon.
Opposite: Feeding an organism as large and heavy as a whale shark (*Rhincodon typus*) is not easy: filtering water lets such seagoing machines locate adequate nutrition.

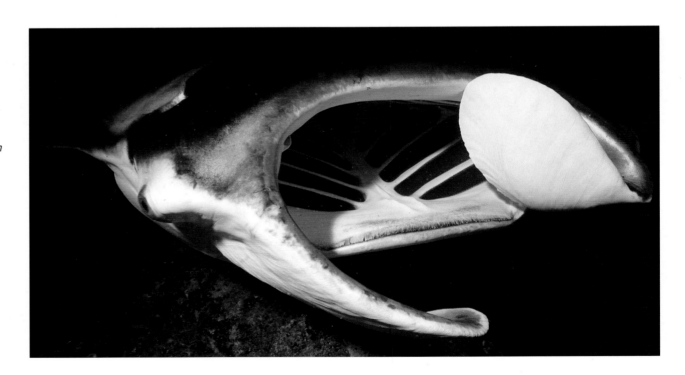

Some sharks are adapted to life on the bottom of the sea and blend in with that environment. Some have colors that help camouflage them, and others have barbels on their snout that disguise their true shape. They pass their entire existence within a small area where they wait to ambush small prey, somewhat like a crocodile in a river; surprise is their primary weapon. The majority of sharks, however, swim in the open water where there are no hiding places to wait in ambush. How do they adapt? Evolution has helped them with a trick: reversed shadows. Most sharks are of a "neutral" color that blends well with sea water: gray, blue, or green, more rarely a dark bronze color. But this is not all. In sunlight, the back of a fish, the side facing the sun, will be paler, while its stomach, being in shadow, will

tend to be darker. The trick, then, is simple: sharks reverse these tonalities to confuse prey as to the true shape of their bodies. Observed from below, the pale underside of a shark can be seen to blend in with the bright surface above; looked at from above, the dark topside of a shark makes it almost disappear against the dark ocean bottom. Sharks are adept at exploiting this camouflage. White sharks (*Carcharodon carcharias*), for example, always swim either near the surface or very close to the bottom, only rarely in the middle of the water.

Most sharks lead a solitary life, swimming and hunting alone. It is true that spectacular concentrations of hundreds of sharks have been observed, particularly in the case of hammerheads (*Sphyrina zygaena*), but these are seasonal groupings probably related to reproduction. Even so, sharks often have "traveling companions." First among these are a host of parasites: crustaceans such as the copepods (sometimes called sea lice), flatworms, roundworms, and so

on. These parasites attach themselves to the shark's fins or skin; some are specialized and prefer gills or even the cornea of an eye. In addition to parasites, many sharks take other fish along with them in their travels: remoras (or suckerfish), for example,

which anchor themselves to the shark's skin with special suckers. There is a tacit agreement between a shark and its remoras: the remoras profit from the food remains from the shark's predations, and the remoras, in turn, eliminate parasites from the

shark's body. Frequently, the remoras end up being devoured by their host. Sharks have other "collaborators," including pilot fish. The oceanic white tip (*Carcharhinus longimanus*), an elegant shark of the open seas with snow-white tips on its fins,

Opposite above: The diver is dressed in protective steel armor; by placing a fish on the back of his hand and extending his arm, he has attracted a shark, which then takes a bite.
Opposite below: The movements a ray performs to catch its prey are truly acrobatic.
Right: A blue shark (*Prionace glauca*) eats its weight in fish every month. Half of this caloric intake goes to keeping the shark healthy and moving, one fourth is used for growth, and one fourth is evacuated.

exploits these traveling companions to hide itself from the view of prey. The small pilot fish swim near its fins or in front of its snout, exploiting the "bow wave" (a little like surfers) created by the shark's movement through the water. Against the blue background of the sea, the big shark disappears amid its small companions and the flashing light.

From a distance, it is practically invisible except for the white tips of its fins, which glint in the light along with the small pilot fish, giving the impression that what is approaching is not a shark, but only a school of small fish. As the shark swims closer, this illusion is confirmed by the presence of the pilot fish. They may not be numerous, but even a small num-

ber will suffice to break up the shark's outline against the background of the sea. When the shark is close enough, it determines whether to attack or to continue examining its prey by making wide circles around it. In fact, this shark is generally cautious and prudent, but when it finally decides to attack its prey, it is deadly.

Below: The fins of an oceanic white tip (*Carcharhinus longimanus*) are black at birth but become white when the shark reaches sexual maturity.
Right: Small fish like these barred jack (*Gnathanodon speciosus*) often take advantage of the wake or bow wave generated by a whale shark (*Rhincodon typus*). Sharks are also host to a great many parasites, including copepods and sea lice, flatworms and roundworms. Some attach themselves to fins or skin, and others get inside gills or even attach to the cornea of the eye.

A stomach of iron

You can find a little bit of everything in the stomach of a large shark: tuna, swordfish, turtles, dolphins, squid, other sharks, and so on. Whenever a shark is fished out of the water, everyone nearby is eager to see the contents of its stomach. Human remains have actually been discovered in the stomachs of sharks, but such occurrences are extremely rare and may have nothing to do with an act of predation; it's always possible that the shark came upon a floating cadaver.

The literature on sharks offers lists of surprising things that have been found in their stomachs. One blue shark (*Prionace glauca*) was found to have consumed one raincoat, three overcoats, and an automobile license plate. The stomachs of other sharks have yielded up bottles, rolls of wallpaper, even a keg of nails. Then there are the historical documents from the harbor officials of Aix, France, which include the report of a fisherman who captured a shark more than 20 feet long (probably a white shark).

Preceding pages, left above: Even birds can fall prey to sharks.
Preceding pages, left below: A single bite by a white shark (Carcharodon carcharias) on an Australian sea lion. The wound is deep enough that the animal will die from loss of blood; rather than risk a battle, the shark waits for the animal to die.
Preceding pages, right: A sea lion in the Galapagos.

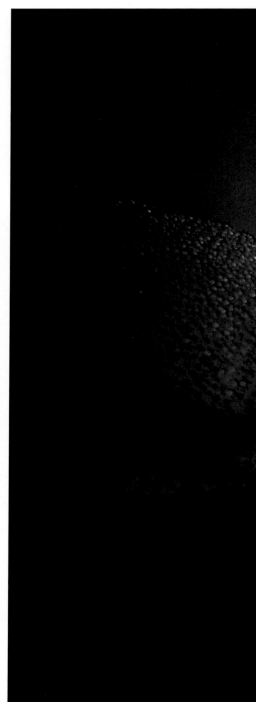

Opposite, above: The remains of an enormous deep-sea octopus (*Haliphron atlanticus*).

Opposite, bottom: Many sharks are generally fond of crustaceans, with a special fondness for lobsters.

Left and below: Egg mass of a giant squid (*Thysanoteuthis rombus*): an important food source, rich in protein, for oceanic sharks like the oceanic white tip (*Carcharhinus longimanus*).

Its stomach contained the headless body of a man in full armor. Incredible! It is a matter of record that sharks will try to consume even indigestible objects, regardless of their size and shape. Underwater telephone cables have been repeatedly damaged, and sharks have

even tried to take bites out of nuclear submarines. Sharks are probably driven to attacking these objects not by nagging hunger, but rather by the magnetic fields they give off. If a shark manages to gulp down something truly indigestible, it can evert its stomach.

The digestive system of sharks is comparatively simple. Along with powerful digestive enzymes and gastric acids, it

Below: As eager to play as a puppy, this young sea lion extends its nose to be petted.
Right: Diving amid sharks in the Bahamas can be a thrilling experience. The visiting divers arrange themselves in a semicircle underwater, kneel in the sand, and wait; then the local guides release fish into the water. As dozens of Caribbean reef sharks (*Carcharhinus perezi*) take off after the bait, the divers watch the spectacle, their amazement tinged with fear.

Left: Few denizens of the deep can threaten the life of a 15-foot pilot whale, but the little cookie-cutter shark (*Isistius brasiliensis*) can certainly cause it more than a little discomfort. The small shark uses its suckerlike lips to attach its mouth to the body of a whale—or a tuna, porpoise, squid, or other shark—and, using its tongue to create a vacuum, it swivels around to bite off a disk of meat with its extremely sharp teeth. The resulting hole, about the size of a cookie, heals in a few days, but the scar remains. One such scar is visible on this whale, on its side near the ·pectoral fin.

involves a specially shaped intestine, similar to the muffler of an automobile. This is the spiral valve, which greatly increases the area used to absorb nutrients from food. Food must pass along the convolutions of the spiral valve before being evacuated through the cloaca.

Left: Turtles are a source of food for sharks, but they also provide nutrition for the fish that free them of parasites.
Below: The tiger shark (*Galeocerdo cuvier*) attacks and eats everything—it is the least selective shark, as well as the most opportunistic. Their stomachs have been found to contain fish, snakes, lobster, mice, other sharks, carcasses of mammals, and turtles, for which it has a particular fondness, piercing their shells with its sharp teeth.

Following pages, left: Blue sharks (*Prionace glauca*) rarely come near beaches since they live primarily on the open seas.
Following pages, right: The beaches of Sydney, Australia, along with much of that country's coastline, are protected by antishark nets like these.

Sharks and people

Taking a swim in the middle of the ocean awakens different sensations in different people. Some find it relaxing, while others experience nothing but dread and fear. Unable to see what is beneath their feet in the blue depths, they sense themselves open to an attack, and the ancestral fear of being devoured by a predator is awakened. How much should we fear sharks? Swimming in the ocean is certainly far safer than traveling by automobile, but a lot depends on where you take the plunge. If you dive into water where there have been repeated instances of shark attacks or where dangerous sharks are known to hunt—well, you may be at risk. Of the more than 370 known species of shark, 90 percent are not dangerous to humans. Even so, species do exist that will attack people, and when it comes to these sharks, avoiding a one-on-one encounter is always the very best idea.

- **Sharkphobia**
- **Protecting people**
- **A predator in danger**

Sharkphobia

According to the International Shark Attack File, there are annually about 50 to 75 shark attacks throughout the world, and of those from 5 to 10 end in a human fatality. Of course, these official statistics do not include information on attacks in third world countries or those that happen following small shipwrecks (local fishing boats, boat people, etc.). Oddly enough, most of the recorded attacks involve a theoretically harmless shark: the nurse shark.

The nurse shark (*Gingly-mostoma cirratum*) is a "peaceful" shark that often rests on the sea bottom; scuba divers like to swim down and pet it or even pull its tail. The predictable result is that the sharks will suddenly turn and bite the divers in self-defense. The highest number of fatal attacks are attributed to the tiger shark (*Galeocerdo cuvier*) and the great white shark (*Carcharodon carcharias*). Their methods of attack are completely different. While the white shark usually bites once and moves off, wait-

ing for the prey to die from loss of blood, the tiger shark makes a devastating attack (it has an enormous mouth), finishing off its victim with a nonstop sequence of bites, one after another. These two sharks have more or less ruined the reputation of all sharks. In many islands of the Pacific and, in general, wherever sharks are well known, they are treated with enormous respect and even love—sometimes they are worshipped as the incarnations of ancestors or spirits. Elsewhere, these carnivorous

fish are treated only with hatred, distrust, and fear. Often the mass media tends to fan the flames of such feelings with blood-curdling reports and scares each time a fin is sighted breaking the surface of water.

Above: A scent trail of blood and ground fish forms an irresistible lure for any shark that crosses it. Hemoglobins and other proteins in the chum will be carried on the currents for miles, and sharks will follow the trail, zigzagging back and forth right up to the boat.
Right: The shark cage has openings for cameras and two large escape hatches to afford speedy exit in case of emergency.

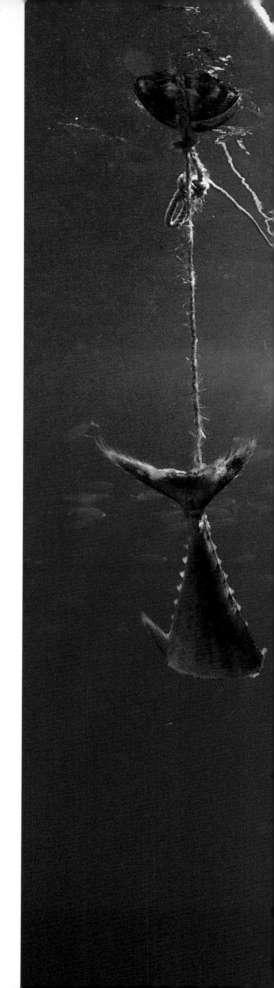

Protecting people

Contrary to popular opinion, meeting up with a shark in the middle of the ocean is really not so easy. This is partly because the number of sharks has been reduced, most drastically in recent years, and partly because sharks are wary and prefer to keep their distance. The dangerous species, in particular, are so rare that experts must often wait weeks and even months before finding one. Then, when they finally spot one of these rare creatures, getting close to it is even more difficult. Hammerheads (*Sphyrina zygaena*), for example, have learned to fear the air bubbles of scuba divers.

Top left: Transmitters come in different types and sizes. The small orange one, hardly larger than a finger, indicates a shark's position by transmitting impulses to a hydrophone; the larger one relates the animal's speed and direction of travel.
Above: There are also simple tags used to identify an animal; the small tag, which is attached to the shark, bears a number keyed to information on a file card.

Should scuba divers take any particular protective measures when diving? In normal situations, and with the vast majority of sharks, no special precautions are called for: sharks are fish like any others (would you climb in a protective cage in the middle of some tuna?). Problems may arise, however, if you're forced to spend a long time in the water, as in the case of a shipwreck or with people who work underwater, or, of course, if you're swimming in waters visited by aggressive sharks.

Opposite top right: A large slice of barracuda is used as bait.

Opposite bottom right: A shark nearly as long as the boat has taken the bait. It will be tagged in the water and released. Since they have no skeletal bones, sharks cannot be taken out of the water, not even for a few seconds: lacking the support of skeletal ribs, they would be crushed by their own weight.

Below: A hydrophone. This is a kind of extremely sensitive artificial ear that picks up impulses from transmitters over a vast area.

Bottom: This tiger shark (*Galeocerdo cuvier*) has just been tagged by Professor Gruber. It will rest on the bottom for only a moment: it must swim in order to breathe.

Left above: A tag with an identification number is attached at the bottom of the dorsal fin. This small injection causes the shark no pain.

Left center: Measuring a small lemon shark (*Negaprion brevirostris*). If this shark is encountered again in a few years, it will be possible to determine its rate of growth, which is not constant: sharks grow rapidly at first, but once they reach a certain size their growth rate slows. As with many other fish and also pythons, sharks continue to grow until they die.

Left bottom: Performing an autopsy on a shark reveals a wealth of information, but animals are never killed for research purposes.

In such cases, it is important to have some system of defense. Which one is best? No single defense system is known to provide sure-fire protection against all sharks all of the time. There are many ways of handling the problem, however, each one more or less useful according to the situation. Spearguns loaded with explosive charges, antishark darts, or CO_2 cylinders must be handled and used with extreme care or they immediately become more dangerous than any shark. Antishark "billy clubs" (wooden clubs with spiked heads) let a diver hold a few sharks at bay—but only a very few at a time. The special inflatable plastic bags that one climbs into like a floating sleeping bag are useful, most of all in cases of shipwreck. These are for survival, however, and they make

Right: The length of the dorsal fin of a whale shark (*Rhincodon typus*) can be used to determine the shark's overall length, which is usually about nine times that of the fin. This specimen, nearly 30 feet long, will have a liver weighing about 1,500 pounds. These sharks live in the warm waters of tropical and subtropical seas; in theory, they could enter the Mediterranean Sea by way of the Suez Canal, but as of yet there have been no reported sightings. Until recently, the method of reproduction used by whale sharks (*Rhincodon typus*) was a mystery: an egg found in the Gulf of Mexico led to the theory that the sharks deposited eggs, but then the uteri of captured female sharks were found to contain live embryos.

movement difficult and cut down on vision. Chemical repellents are useful only with certain species, and they have the great defect of rapidly dispersing in water. Metal cages for divers are safe, but require a great deal of organization (and are thus impractical in the case of shipwrecks). Chain-mail-style metal armor works only with small or medium-size sharks; it is not effective against large sharks, and it is useless in the presence of those sharks (such as makos) that have highly pointed teeth. The POD is the only system that seems to have a certain large-scale efficacy. This is a portable electric device designed by the South African government that generates an electric charge over a distance of about ten feet. Ron and Valerie Taylor, Australian photographers and film makers,

Left: Ron and Valerie Taylor, together with Ian Gordon, are testing out the POD, a device that creates electric impulses that disturb sharks' sensory organs (the ampullae of Lorenzini). The device has been found to provide useful protection against even white sharks (*Carcharodon carcharias*), which turned back when given an electric "punch" from a distance of about ten feet. In performing these experiments, the three Australians have shown more than a little courage and composure.
Below left: The device can be seen here mounted on a diver's air tank; the diver holds the wand.

have tested it with success on all the most dangerous species of shark (including the white shark). It does not work with the oceanic white tip (*Carcharhinus longimanus*).

It has been determined that no particular bathing suit or other article of clothing will attract or repel sharks in water. Sharks do, however, respond to colors, and lively and luminous colors seem to attract sharks far more than less striking ones. Some researchers claim that the white shark (*Carcharodon carcharias*) is particularly drawn to the color yellow. As has been said, shark attacks on humans, though rare, are possible in all the world's oceans and seas (except for Antarctica, where

Right: The jaws of a great white shark (*Carcharodon carcharias*) can cut a human in half; the scientific name Carcharodon means "sharp teeth." According to experiments conducted by Paul Atkins on the Farallon Islands off San Francisco: after eating an elephant seal weighing more than 400 pounds, the shark will spend several weeks digesting (some researchers would claim as long as three months). The shark's large liver is an important source of nourishment between meals.
Below: Even inside a shark cage, a distracted or incautious gesture can be dangerous.

no sharks have been seen or captured—which, however, does not rule out the possibility of some species living there).

Sharks have not been a subject of scientific study for very long; only recently have developments in underwater equipment made such studies possible. Researchers are concentrating primarily on certain aspects of shark physiology and behavior. Scientists are investigating the extraordinary sensory abilities of sharks and their enormous ability to adapt to very different environmental conditions. Recently, much attention has been focused on sharks' presumed invulnerability to tumors. In reality, sharks, like all animals, are susceptible to cancer. The fact that cancer rarely develops excessively may be because as soon as it appears, the shark quickly loses its efficiency as a predator, weakens, and soon dies from natural causes. Unfortunately, unscrupulous people are seeking to exploit this myth to sell antitumor products composed of various shark ingredients. For the past few years interesting studies have been conducted on the denticles that cover the bodies of sharks. They apparently permit sharks to swim with less friction by channeling water over the shark's body in minuscule rivulets at its sides in order to minimize turbulence. Some researchers have considered the possibility of covering airplanes with artificial "shark-skin," designed by computer to cut down on friction. This would theoretically save fuel and create less pollution.

If there is a shark that can be easily approached it is the oceanic white tip (*Carcharhinus longimanus*): as soon as it senses the presence of a possible prey, it turns and goes in that direction, slowly but without hesitation. If driven off, it will just turn and come right back. After a few minutes it's a good idea to get out of the water.

A predator in danger

Millions of sharks are killed every year (nearly a half million in the United States alone). They are fished for their skin, for sport, and killed accidentally. The major threat to sharks, however, is Oriental cooking. The traditional shark-fin soup (made from the fin of the white), for example, is literally causing the extermination of the shark population throughout the world.

As a result, fishermen exploit the market by cutting the fins off sharks: the most highly valued are those of the white shark (*Carcharodon carcharias*), which can bring up to several hundred dollars a pound. To satisfy the tastes of restaurant patrons, one of the most terrifying slaughters in the history of the animal world is being carried out on a universal scale. This commercial enterprise is made even crueler by the practice of "finning," or cutting the fins off a shark and then tossing it back into the water—alive but destined to meet a truly atro-

cious death. "Finned" sharks die from slow suffocation caused by their inability to swim—if they can't swim they can't take in water and oxygen. Or else they die of hunger because they are no longer able to take prey.

As of yet, little has been done

Far left: An eagle ray trapped and dying in fishing nets in the Mediterranean Sea.
Above: This tropical ray (*Taeniura lymma*) has lost its tail in a violent attack, but it will survive.
Left: A blue shark (*Prionace glauca*) caught during a fishing contest in the Adriatic Sea. Because it has a low value in terms of points, it will be marked and released.

to put a stop to this slaughter. Enormous efforts have been made to save the panda, the condor, and the whale, but the same is not yet true of sharks. Perhaps this is because of their reputation as man-eaters, but the same is true of the wolf and the Siberian tiger, which today have become prominent symbols of the movement to protect wildlife and nature. We must hope that the movement to stop this slaughter will get under way before it is too late. For if the slaughter continues unabated, sharks will soon be so rare as to become curiosities. Unfortunately, there is already a troubling precedent. Although the mass media have generally remained silent on the subject, a famous fish, a close relative of the shark (some forms

"are" sharks), is in the process of disappearing: the sawfish. It has already become virtually extinct. Will the same thing happen to the shark?

Actually, something is being done. The white shark (*Carcharodon carcharias*) has already been declared a protected species in California, southeastern Australia, the Maldives, and South Africa. It is protected by rules similar to those that protect elephants and their ivory: no parts of the shark's body can be sold. The protocol of the Barcelona Convention (February 1975) bans the capture and commerce of white sharks (*Carcharodon carcharias*), basking sharks (*Cetorhinus maximus*), and devilfish (the genus *Mobula* of the Mediterranean). The same accord seeks to regulate the fishing of other sharks, such as the blue shark (*Prionace glauca*), porbeagle (*Lamna nasus*), and mako (*Isurus oxyrinchus*). Naturally, each of

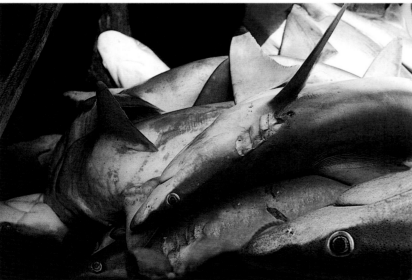

Above left: A thresher shark (*Alopias vulpinus*) displayed as a trophy. The thresher is a member of the lamniforms, the group that includes the mako (*Isurus oxyrinchus*) and great white shark (*Carcharodon carcharias*). It uses its long tail to frighten and herd small fish.
Left: Large-scale slaughters are being committed in the collection of shark fins, which sell at high prices in the Orient. In many cases, the sharks, alive or dead, are thrown back onto the water after their fins have been cut off. Fishermen do this to avoid using up valuable storage space on board their ships.
Right: A restaurant that specializes in shark fin. This food fad has led to the widespread commerce in shark fins.
Opposite: Every species of shark has suffered diminished numbers recently, and the white shark (*Carcharodon carcharias*) is in danger of extinction. More are begin taken than are being born. Their highly evolved reproductive system was not able to foresee the coming of humans.

the signatory countries will have to ratify the accord, translating it into national laws, but there is every reason to believe that this can be done.

Elsewhere in the world, there are shops selling shark teeth, as well as entire jaws, at incredible prices: hundreds of dollars for a single tooth; a jaw in good condition can bring several thousand. The real problem is that little is known about the true situation of the various shark populations of the world. It takes many years for a shark to reach sexual maturity, which means that it would be impossible for sharks to repopulate the world's oceans if the current rate of killing is allowed to continue. For the first time in 400 million years of evolution, the very survival of sharks is threatened. The only hope for their survival must come from their "human predators." Movements to protect them have already begun, but time is running out.

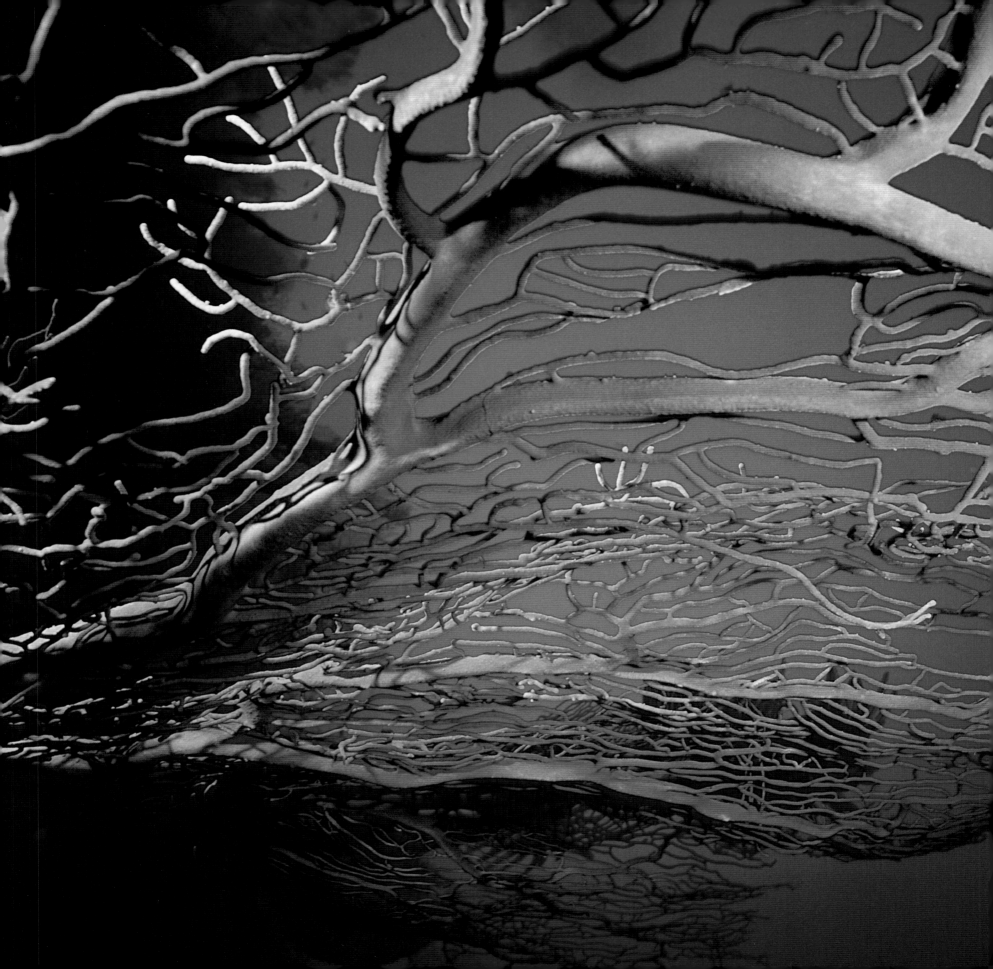

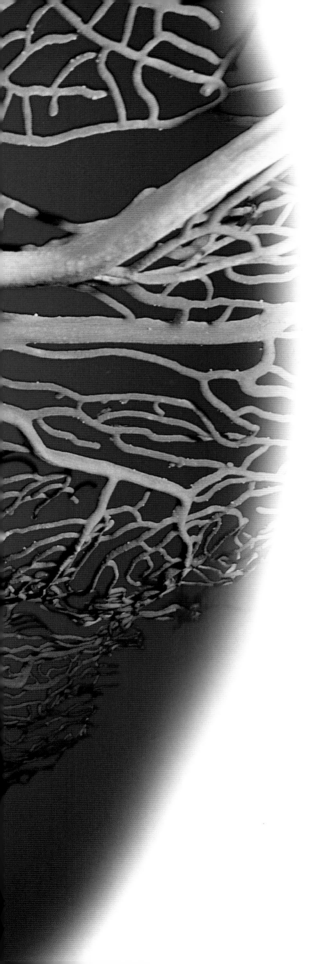

Once upon a time

Sharks are the product of a long evolution, one that has been in progress for hundreds of millions of years. In all that time the general shape of their bodies has never changed, nor have their predatory habits. A few alterations have been made, but always very minor ones. All of the principal groups of today's sharks appeared about 100 million years ago during the age of dinosaurs. The sharks alive today are faithful representatives of the ancestral "formula." Indeed, sharks are among the few currently living creatures to remain anchored to the same evolutionary formula. The same could not be said, for example, of the other fish whose ancestors swam in those primordial seas alongside sharks. Over the same span of time, those fish have gone through a spectacular transformation, changing not just their physiology but also the environment in which they live. Many became lunged fish, then amphibians, then reptiles, and then birds or mammals.

- **Distant origins**
- **What remains**

Distant origins

From the point of view of evolution, there's really very little to say about sharks. It's far more correct to refer to Elasmobranchii, the group to which sharks belong, along with rays and torpedoes. These fish, so very different in appearance today, share a single ancestor that swam in the seas between the Silurian and Devonian periods about 400 million years ago.

At some point along the evolutionary chain, the Elasmobranchii became joined to the group of the chimaera, cartilaginous marine fish still living in temperate oceans throughout the world. The Elasmobranchii enjoyed enormous success during the Carboniferous period about 360 million years ago, but then went through a period of crisis, probably as a result of competition with other marine creatures. During the age of the dinosaurs they experienced another period of great success;

it was then that sharks assumed their modern forms. It is interesting to note that for hundreds of millions of years the form of the Elasmobranchii has remained, so to speak, "standard." Only during the age of the dinosaurs, particularly in the Jurassic period, did some forms begin to "go flat," leading eventually to today's rays, torpedoes, guitarfish, and sawfish. Although denticles and isolated teeth have been found in rocks from even earlier periods, the most important fossil remains are without doubt those of the

Preceding pages, left: A coral formation of gorgonia.
Preceding pages, right: The magic of a dawn at sea.

Above: The eye of a manta (*Manta birostris*).
Right: Sea urchins are a favorite food of many bottom-dwelling sharks, such as the nurse shark (*Ginglymostoma cirratum*) and Port Jackson shark (*Heterodontus portus jacksoni*), two of the oldest species.

Opposite: The nautilus is the sole survivor of a group that flourished 200 million years ago. It is a carnivore and lives in deep water.

Right: This fearsome tooth, shown here at close to life size (the average is about 5 inches), belonged to a megalodon (*Carcharocles megalodon*), a monster shark that lived between 20 million and 2 million years ago. Until recently, this fossil shark was included in the genus Carcharodon, the same as the great white shark (*Carcharodon carcharias*), but a new classification has changed the nomenclature of this group. This ancient shark is thought to have reached a length of about 45 feet.

Cladoselache, a shark that lived about 380 million years ago. Specimens of this shark have been found in rock strata in Ohio, Kentucky, and Tennessee. The remains found by paleontologists are so well preserved that they resemble fossil X-rays. One can see clearly the outline of the shark's entire body, with its skin, muscles, cartilaginous bones, teeth, and even kidneys. Its shape is that typical of a shark, with several variations: the mouth was not on the underside of the body but at the end of the snout, as with a trout, giving its head a more solid appearance. It preyed on cephalopods, crustaceans, and small primitive bony fish. All in all, the Cladoselache, about six feet long, was a powerful ocean predator. A predator, however, that often ended up in the jaws of other even larger carnivores, such as the large placoderms, truly monstrous armored fish.

The evolutionary story of the Cladoselache ends with the end of the Carboniferous period, about 290 million years ago. At that time dinosaurs did not yet exist, but Earth's next "stars" were already swimming in the planet's seas: the Ibodontidi. Their habits and appearance were so similar to those of modern sharks that some paleontologists refer to them today as "the blue sharks of prehistory." These shark forms were the first in the fossil record to exhibit claspers, the male reproductive organs, along with other traits.

Petrified remains offer various curiosities. The genus Hybodus, for example, had two very different kinds of teeth: sharp, in front, and flat, almost like small domes, behind. Evidently this shark was able not only to tear flesh but also to chew up bones and the shells of mollusks; an omnivorous characteristic that must have contributed to its great success in its time.

The sudden disappearance of the Ibodontidi sharks along with the dinosaurs 65 million years ago opened the way for the modern sharks. One witness to this extraordinary evolution is another predator, equally ancient and primitive, that still lives in the blues waters of today's seas: the nautilus. In fact, for millions of years it has been a "traveling companion" of the shark. Today it lives in the

Right: The humpback whale. This giant megalodon almost certainly preyed on the ancestors of today's whales and those attacks must have been devastating. The jaws of megalodons are reconstructed in museum displays all over the world (quite often at slightly exaggerated sizes).Prehistoric seas were anything but peaceful when this ferocious shark roamed in search of prey. It became extinct without leaving descendants, which in some ways may be fortunate.

shadows of the abyss and comes to the surface only at night, when it hunts prey. Encountering one means making a leap back in time and returning to the epoch in which some of its close relatives, the ammonites, were the true rulers of the sea; even more than the sharks. The asteroid or comet that marked the end of the dinosaurs also killed off these cephalopods and relegated the nautilus to the abyss. For their part, sharks suffered fewer losses. In addition to the Ibodontidi sharks, all the fresh-water sharks (they'd colonized rivers and lakes!) disappeared. However, the evolutionary branch of the shark, creatures with enormous adaptive capacities, survived this catastrophe to continue their long history. Today, sharks account for only 3 percent of fish, but, according to the American researcher Lund, during the Carboniferous period they made up all of 60 percent of all species of fish.

What remains

There is relatively little to study in terms of fossil sharks, for sharks are a little like jellyfish in one important way: when they die, they leave behind few traces of themselves. A shark's body has no hard bones like ours (or like those of a dinosaur)—it has only flexible bones made of cartilage. So after a shark dies and its muscles and organs dissolve, its bones eventually disappear too. But there *is* something that remains: its teeth (and to a lesser extent—disks of vertebrae, the denticles of its skin, the occasional spine, etc.). Thus, if you happened to bury a shark in your backyard and returned a few million years later to dig it up, you'd probably find only a little heap of fossilized teeth.

Sifting through the sands of prehistoric sea beds in Colorado, scientists recently discovered traces of what seems to be the oldest known shark. These traces include minuscule denticles, the toothlike structures found in the hides of sharks. The age of these remains is truly astonishing: they are around 450 million years old. The paleontologists found no teeth, however, perhaps because this ancient shark had not yet developed the fearsome jaws of its modern-day descendants.

Every part of a shark's body is the result of a long evolutionary transformation. It is as though nature had been conducting "tests" over hundreds of millions of years, making continuous changes and improvements to every "piece" of this fish, modifying it to help it adjust to meet the needs of the environment of that particular moment. As the result, when we

Above: Microscopic enlargement of the skin of a shark. Sharks do not have scales like fish, but instead rather hard denticles that are ridged to allow water to pass smoothly over them. Sharks have been struggling to survive for millions of years. Many types of shark eat similar prey but different species are able to survive because they inhabit different geographical areas. This is true in the case of the blue shark (*Prionace glauca*) (right) and the oceanic white tip (*Carcharhinus longimanus*), both of which are open-sea predators; but the first hunts in temperate waters, the second in tropical.

find ourselves facing a shark today, even if the encounter takes place in a fish market, we are looking at a highly sophisticated product of evolution. Most of all in terms of the "raw materials," so to speak.

Traditionally, people have found uses for nearly every part of a shark's body. The meat is very nutritious and can be cooked in many ways: fried, marinated, in soup. For many years, the meat of a certain shark was one of the main ingredients in the famous English dish of fish-and-chips. Other parts of the flesh have been ground up and used as poultry feed and fertilizer (fish meal).

The rest of the shark has been transformed into an aston-ishing variety of products. Shark-liver oil (squalene) was once an important source of vitamin A (today it is more economical to make it synthetically in laboratories). It is still used in cosmetics, as a paint base, a lubricant in aeronautics, an anticoagulant, and even as a treatment for high cholesterol. Shark cartilage has been used for therapeutic purposes (an ointment to treat burns), and shark corneas, along with corneal liquid, have been used in transplants. The skin has been used as a sandpaper called shagreen, also tanned to make a durable leather used in belts and purses. The jaws of sharks have been hung on walls as trophies, and the teeth have been

Sharks produce and lose teeth constantly and have been doing so for more than 400 million years. That fact, and the fact that these teeth are about the only hard parts of a shark's body, are why teeth are the most common shark fossils. A single blue shark (*Prionace glauca*) (above) goes through several thousand teeth in the course of its life, and since there are hundreds of millions of sharks alive today, a lot of teeth are being lost. The horn shark (*Heterodontus francisci*) (left) is one of the oldest existing species.

Opposite: The jaws of vertebrates and sharks are a result of evolution. In fact, jaws are a result of changes in ancient gill arches, the structures that support gill slits. Over the course of evolution, the first of these arches moved forward and became transformed, leading to the origin of the upper jaw and the mandible. Naturally, along the way the sharks came by their teeth. These belong to a sand tiger (*Eugomphodus taurus*).

used to make arrowheads and necklaces. Shark blood has been used to make anticoagulants, and in some parts of the world the spinal column is used to make walking sticks. Perhaps without your knowing it, one of these, or some other object made using shark, may have made its way into your life, directly or indirectly. For centuries sharks have been caught and killed, but it is only recently—and this must be stressed—that this killing has reached the level of a massacre, a true extermination of an ancient being. Today, after hundreds of millions of years of evolution, this predator risks disappearing forever.

We have done our best in this book to present the true face of sharks, not the one so sadly distorted by the mass media and superstition. Today, sharks truly need our help if they are to have any future at all, and the only way to help them is to promote actions aimed at ending this useless slaughter and to show respect for the environment in which sharks live (alongside a vast number of other species of fish, mollusks, and other living creatures). If this does not happen in the next few years, we will see the demise of one of the most fascinating predators that nature has ever produced. In the event of the extinction of the shark, a half billion years of evolution would come to an end.

Bibliography

Angela, Piero and Alberto. *Dentro il Mediterraneo*. Milan: Arnoldo Mondadori, 1995.

Budker, Paul, and P. J. Whitehead. *The Life of Sharks* (trans., rev ed.). London: Weidenfeld and Nicholson, 1971.

Cafiero, Gaetano, and Maddalena Jahoda. *Giants of the Sea* (trans. by Anthony Shuggar). Shrewsbury, England: Swan Hill Press, 1994.

Castro, J. I. *The Sharks of North American Waters*. College Station: Texas A. & M. University Press, 1996.

Cleave, A. *Sharks: A Portrait of the Animal World*. New York: TODTRI, 1994.

Coleman, N. *Australia's Sharks and Rays*. Sydney: Weldon Publishing, 1992.

Compagno, Leonard J. V. *Sharks of the World*. Rome: FAO Species Catalogue, 1984.

Coppleson, Victor Marcus. *Shark Attack*. Sydney: Angus and Robertson, 1962.

Coupe, S. R. *Sharks*. New York: Weldon Owen Pty Ltd., 1990.

Cousteau, J. Y., and P. Cousteau. *The Shark: Splendid Savage of the Seas*. London: Cassell, 1970.

Cousteau, Jean-Michel, and Mose Richards. *Cousteau's Great White Shark*. New York: Harry N. Abrams, 1992.

Discovering Sharks. Highlands: American Littoral Society, 1991.

Ellis, Richard. *The Book of Sharks*. New York: Alfred Knopf, 1989.

Ellis, Richard, and John E. McCosker. *Great White Shark*. New York: Harper Collins Publishers, 1991.

Farino, T. *Sharks*. London: Tiger Books International, 1993.

Greenberg, K. E. *Marine Biologist*. Woodbridge: Blackbirch Press, 1996.

Hall, M. and H. *The Shark Project Book*. London: Hodder & Stoughton Children's Books, 1993.

Hawke, K. *The Tiger Shark*. Melbourne: MacMillan Education, 1994.

Johnson, R. H. *Sharks of Polynesia*. Singapore: Les Editions du Pacifique, 1978.

Klimley, A. P., and D. G. Ainley. *Great White Sharks*. San Diego: Academic Press, 1996.

Last, P. R., and J. D. Stevens. *Sharks and Rays of Australia*. Hobart: CSIRO, 1994.

Lawrence, R. D. *Shark! Nature's Masterpiece*. Vermont: Chapters Publishing Ltd., 1985.

Lineaweaker, T. H., and R. H. Backus. *The Natural History of Sharks*. Philadelphia: J. B. Lippincott Company, 1970.

Maniguet, Xavier. *The Jaws of Death* (trans. by David A. Christie). Dobbs Ferry, N.Y.: Sheridan House, 1994.

Matthews, D. *Sharks!* Maryland: Discovery Channel Book, 1996.

Perrine, D. *Sharks*. Stillwater: Voyageur Press, 1995.

Pope, P. E. *A Dictionary of Sharks*. 1973.

Randall, J. E. *Sharks of Arabia*. London: Immel Publishing, 1986.

Resnick. J. *Sharks!* Bridgeport: Third Story Books.

Snyderman, M. *Shark: Endangered Predator of the Sea*. Toronto: Key Poerter Books, 1995.

Springer, V. G., and J. P. Gold. *Sharks in Question*. Washington, D.C.: Smithsonian Institution Press, 1989.

Stafford-Deitsch, J. *Shark: A Photographer's Story*. San Francisco: Sierra Club books, 1988.

Steel, Rodney. *Sharks of the World*. New York: Facts On File, 1985.

Stevens, John D., ed. *Sharks*. New York: Facts On File, 1987.

Taylor, G. *Whale Sharks*. Sydney: Angus & Robertson, 1994.

Taylor, L. R. *Sharks of Hawaii*. Honolulu: University of Hawaii Press, 1993.

Taylor, R. and V., et al. *Sharks: Silent Hunters of the Deep*. Surry Hills: Reader's Digest Services Pty Ltd., 1987.

Acknowledgments

The photographs in this book are the fruit of years of diving in oceans all over the world, along sea floors and in caves, in cold water and warm, by day and by night, and in aquariums and scientific laboratories. Certain results can be achieved only through teamwork, and this was one. I had the good fortune to be able to count on friends who offered generous help, both in the water and on dry land. They gave me information, news, suggestions, and assistance; together we shared many experiences, many dives, a great deal of work—and countless rolls of film.

Bob and Cathy Cranston, Howard and Michelle Hall, Paul Humann, Samuel and Marie Gruber, Salvatore Braca, Stuart Cove, Ron and Valerie Taylor, Steve Drogin, James Watt, David Fleetham, Ian Gordon, Paul Anes, Dean Grubbs, Julien Zaragoza, Alfred Li, Becca Saunders, Mark Spencer, Marty Synderman, the Bahamas Tourist Office, Vincenzo Lamorgese, Rachael Mackenzie, Bonnie Carini, Cristina Cazzani, Big Game Fishing, Michelangela Vismara, Luigi Marengo, Aldo Lucarelli and Gianfilippo Coletta, Lulo Tognola, Adrienne Barman, Monja Camponovo, Dunja Cometti, Stefano Polli, Maurizio Sciarini, Filippo Vannini, Antonio Stancato, Equipe Sub, Elwyn Gates, and Caterina, Claudia, and Carolina Recchi.

Thanks,   Alberto Luca Recchi

The magnificent dozen

Oceanic white-tip (*Carcharhinus longimanus*)
Lives on high seas in warm waters of tropics. Swims slowly on the surface, often accompanied by pilot fish. Very aggressive—this is the principal danger to shipwreck survivors and survivors of planes crashes. It can exceed 12 feet in length.

Mako (*Isurus oxyrinchus*)
Aggressive, unpredictable in its attacks, exploits its blinding speed to capture fast prey like tuna and bluefish. Meeting this torpedo with its pointed teeth and fixed black eye is an unforgettable experience. Makos can reach 12 feet in length. Because of their speed and leaping ability they have been known to leap into fishing boats—makos are considered an exciting game fish by sport fishermen.

Silvertip (*Carcharhinus albimarginatus*)
Lives in the Pacific and Indian oceans, usually in deep water or near reefs far from the coast. Does not perform long migrations. Gives birth to from one to eleven young after a gestation period of twelve months. Rarely exceeds 8 feet in length. Although swift, aggressive, and opportunistic in seeking prey, it is not particularly dangerous to humans.

Whale shark (*Rhincodon typus*)
The world's largest fish; in fact, the largest cold-blooded animal on the planet. An adult can be as long as a bus and can weigh 20 tons. Is absolutely harmless to humans, since, like the basking shark and manta, it primarily eats plankton and small fish that it sucks in while swimming with its mouth open. Very long-lived.

Great white shark (*Carcharodon carcharias*)
The most fearsome shark because of its lethal jaws, which it uses to slice through large fish and mammals. The stomach of one adult was found to contain 4 large sea lions. The females, larger than the males, can exceed 15 feet in length. This shark has become rare and is protected by many nations. The largest specimen (20 feet) was found in the Mediterranean Sea.

Lemon shark (*Negaprion breviostris*)
Lives in tropical seas, in lagoons, and near coastlines. Changes teeth every week, can exceed 11 feet, and lives up to 80 years. Professor Samuel H. Gruber of the University of Miami, who has studied them for over thirty years, has shown that lemon sharks are able to make associations and remember, much like laboratory mice.

Great hammerhead (*Sphyrna mokarran*)
In the history of shark evolution, the hammerhead is a relative newcomer. Thanks to its large nose, it has a powerful sense of smell. Its mouth is relatively small, and it eats primarily rays. It can reach 20 feet in length, and gives birth to about forty young every two years.

Nurse shark (*Ginglymostoma cirratum*)
Spends most of the time on the floor of tropical and subtropical seas, where it hunts primarily invertebrates like squid and cuttlefish. Although it does not normally attack humans, it holds the record for underwater attacks since it is often molested. It sometimes sucks prey out of cavities in reefs, but its name comes from the old word *nusse,* meaning "large fish." Grows to 12 feet.

Tiger shark (*Galeocerdo cuvier*)
It abounds in the tropics, prefers turbid water, and comes very near shore. Hunts day and night, and its victims can include humans since it is not selective in its eating habits (it has been called a "garbage can with fins"). With its enormous mouth it devours everything: fish, birds, sharks, mice, turtles, various carcasses, even dogs that play too far out in the surf.

Sand shark (*Eugomphodus taurus*)
This shark's hooked teeth, perfect for grasping small fish and squid, add to the fearsome appearance of its snout. It is not known to attack humans. The embryo in the uterus devours other fertilized eggs.

Bull or Zambezi shark (*Carcharhinus leucas*)
Found in the temperate waters of Asia, Africa, America, and Australia. Adapts to lakes and swims many miles up rivers, even the Mississippi. It is stocky and gray, with very small eyes, and easily exceeds 10 feet in length. Like the tiger shark, it eats everything: other sharks, rays, fish, birds, invertebrates, and mammals, including humans. The bull shark, tiger shark, and great white are called the "unholy trinity" because of their attacks on humans.

Blue shark (*Prionace glauca*)
An elegant swimmer of the high seas that lives in temperate and tropical waters all around the world. It reaches 15 feet in length and prefers squid, which it captures even at great depths. It attacks after circling its prey and is potentially dangerous to humans, particularly victims of shipwrecks and plane crashes.

Index of names

Numbers in italics refer to pages with illustrations.

Alopias vulpinus. See thresher shark
bamboo shark, *78*
banjo shark, *20*
barred jack, *100*
basking shark, 95, 125
black-tipped reef shark, 78
blue shark, 17, 38, *41*, 52, *54, 57*, 63, 71, *72, 80, 87, 93*, 99, 102, *109*, 123, 125, *134, 136*, 139
blue-spotted bamboo shark, *31, 82*
bull shark, 17, 18, 139
Caribbean reef shark, *10, 17, 28*, 66, *106*
Carcharhinus albimarginatus. See silvertip shark
Carcharhinus amblyrhynchoides. See Queensland shark
Carcharhinus amblyrhynchos. See gray reef shark
Carcharhinus leucas. See bull shark
Carcharhinus longimanus. See oceanic white tip
Carcharhinus perezi. See Caribbean reef shark
Carcharocles megalodon. See megalodon
Carcharodon carcharias. See great white shark
carpet shark, *28, 34, 85, 90*
Cetorhinus maximus. See basking shark

Chiloscyllium caerulopunctatum. See blue-spotted bamboo shark
chimaera, 28, 128
Cladoselache, 128, 131, 132
cookie-cutter shark, *108*
copepods, 99, *103*
Dasyatis sp. *See* stingray
devilfish (genus *Mobula*), 125
dolphin, 18, *39*
eagle ray, *34, 78, 96, 123*
Elasmobranchii, 28, 128
Galeocerdo cuvier. See tiger shark
giant squid, *105*
Ginglymostoma cirratum. See nurse shark
Gnathanodon speciosus. See barred jack
gray reef shark, 20, 78
great hammerhead, 17, 139
great white shark, *14*, 17, *22, 24, 25, 30, 34, 37, 38, 41*, 42, *45*, 52, *64*, 66, *71, 72, 85, 87, 88, 93, 96*, 99, *104*, 112, *118, 119*, 123, 124, 125, *131*, 139
guitarfish, *90*, 128
gummy shark, *66*
Haliphron atlanticus. See octopus
hammerhead, *41*, 42, *46*, 71, *87, 88*, 99, 114
Heterodontus portus jacksoni. See Port Jackson shark
Holocephali. *See* chimaera
Horn shark, *69, 99*
humpback whale, *132*
Ibodontidi, 132
Isistius brasiliensis. See cookie-cutter shark

Isurus oxyrinchus. See mako
lemon shark, *28, 54, 60, 80, 115*, 139
Lorenzini, ampullae of, *64, 77, 87, 118*
mako, 17, *24*, 34, 50, *52*, 66, *85, 96*, 118, *124*, 125, 139
manta, *18, 37, 41, 96*, 128
Manta birostris. See manta
megalodon, *131, 132*
Mose sole, 93
Mustelus antarcticus. See gummy shark
Mustelus mustelus. See smoothhound
Myliobatis sp. *See* sea eagle
nautilus, *131*, 132
Negaprion brevirostris. See lemon shark
Notorynchus cepedianus. See Tasmanian seven-gill shark
nurse shark, 17, *78*, 112, *136*, 139
oceanic white tip, *10*, 17, *18*, 41, 42, *46*, 99, *100*, 118, *120, 134*, 139
octopus, *105*
Odontaspis taurus. See sand tiger
Orectolobus ornatus. See carpet shark
Pardachirus marmoratus. See Moses sole
pilot fish, 99
pilot whale, 108
porbeagle, 17, 125
Port Jackson shark, *69, 128*
Prionace glauca. See blue shark
Queensland shark, 20
rays, *33, 34, 36, 82, 96*, 99, 128
remoras, *69*, 99
rete mirabilia, 52
Rhincodon typus. See whale shark
sand tiger, *28, 32, 33, 36*, 66, *69*, 71, *74, 136*, 139

sawfish, 124, 128
Schneider, folds of, 78
seals, *96*
sea lice, *100*
sea lions, *96, 104, 106*
sea urchins, 128
silvertip shark, *78*, 139
smoothhound, *69*
Sphyrina mokarran. See great hammerhead
Sphyrina zygaena. See hammerhead
stingray, *17*, 66
suckerfish. *See* remoras
swellshark, *10, 72*
Taeniura lymma. See tropical ray
tapetum lucidum, 82
Tasmanian seven-gill shark, *37*
thresher shark, 18, 52, *96*, 124
Thysanothanthis rombus. See giant squid
tiger shark, *10*, 17, *54*, 63, 66, *93, 109*, 112, *115*, 139
tope, 17
torpedos (electric rays), 128
Triaenodon obesus. See white-tip reef shark
tropical ray, *33, 123*
Trygonorrhina sp. A. *See* banjo shark
turtle, *109*
whale shark, *10*, 17, *21, 32, 33, 34, 35, 36, 41*, 42, *45, 46, 57*, 63, *85*, 95, *96, 100, 116*, 139
white shark. *See* great white shark
white-tip reef shark, 33, 93
wobbegong. *See* carpet shark